JACK OF ALL TRADES

JACK McKEON
WITH TOM FRIEND

CB

CONTEMPORARY
BOOKS

CHICAGO · NEW YORK

Library of Congress Cataloging-in-Publication Data

McKeon, Jack.
   Jack of all trades / Jack McKeon with Tom Friend.
      p.   cm.
   ISBN 0-8092-4619-8
   1. McKeon, Jack.   2. Baseball—United States—
   Managers—Biography.
I. Friend, Tom.   II. Title.
GV865.M39A3   1988
796.357'092'4—dc19
[B]   87-36496
                                    CIP

Published by Contemporary Books, Inc.
180 North Michigan Avenue, Chicago, Illinois 60601
Manufactured in the United States of America
Library of Congress Catalog Card Number: 87-36496
International Standard Book Number: 0-8092-4619-8

Published simultaneously in Canada by Beaverbooks, Ltd.
195 Allstate Parkway, Valleywood Business Park
Markham, Ontario L3R 4T8 Canada

This book is dedicated to my wonderful wife, Carol, who has provided inspiration, support, and love for thirty-three years, and to my children, Kristi, Kelly, Kori, and Kasey, for their love and understanding, and to my grandchildren, Zack, Kellan, and Braylee, for making me feel young again.

—Jack McKeon

To John Boggs; to Bill Beck; and, of course, to Jack, for giving me Geritol; and to Diane Murray, for giving me inspiration.

—Tom Friend

Contents

When I managed, I didn't like it when my players got hurt. If someone got hit in the wrist with a pitch, I'd run out, spit some of my tobacco juice on his wrist, and rub it in. It's amazing how many guys shook off their injuries once I started spitting on them.

1
Get Off Your Duff
(I'm Always Off Mine)

TAKE SOME GERITOL and read this book. Don't sit on the couch watching "Gilligan's Island." Don't sleep in past 8 A.M. Get going! Get outta bed! Get a job! And read this!

Some people think I'm pushy, but I'm just Trader Jack. I trade for a living. I don't trade stocks and I don't trade bonds, but I trade Terry Kennedy and Ozzie Smith and Kevin McReynolds. I trade just about any ballplayer I get my hands on.

Don't get me wrong. I don't trade just to get my name in the papers. I trade so I can win ball games. Everybody in baseball wants to win, but not everybody in baseball wants to trade. Here's what I mean: At the 1983 winter meetings, I wanted second baseman Frank White of the Royals. The Royals said they'd trade him to me, but they didn't like anybody on my team, the San Diego Padres.

But I take Geritol. I don't sleep in past 8 A.M.

7

I did some sniffing and found out that the Royals liked Bill Buckner, who was then with the Cubs. I talked to the Cubs and found out I could get Buckner for pitcher Dennis Rasmussen. I went back to the Royals and said, "Let's make a deal." I was gonna get Buckner for Rasmussen, and then I was gonna give away Buckner to the Royals, along with second baseman Juan Bonilla and a fringe pitcher, for White and pitcher Frank Wills. The Royals agreed but their general manager John Schuerholz came back later and said, "Can't. They'll run us out of town."

Now listen. John Schuerholz and the Royals have done a hell of a job. They lured Bo Jackson away from football, they won a world title, and a lot more. But you don't worry about getting run out of town, not if you can help your team, right?

I once traded Ozzie Smith.

Enough said.

Nothing against baseball people, but my point is you need guts in this business. You gotta take risks. You gotta get off your duff. Listen, I hardly missed a game when I played. In case you missed my career, I played eight years in the minor leagues in such places as Greenville, Alabama, and Burlington, North Carolina, and Missoula, Montana. I was a fat catcher who hit three ways: right, left, and seldom. My career average was around .300: .150 from the right side and .150 from the left. You couldn't get me out of the lineup. One day when I was catching in Pittsfield, Massachusetts, Brooks Lawrence—who later ended up pitching for the Reds—swung and dribbled a ball right in front of me. I pounced on it. In fact, I was so quick that Lawrence's bat hit me smack in the forehead on his follow through. It was a pretty bad cut. Women passed out in the stands. They rushed me to the hospital and sewed me up with eight stitches. The doctors said I had to stay overnight for observation, but they failed to observe me sneaking out of the hospital a few hours later.

The next morning, I boarded the team bus like always. I couldn't play, but I wasn't going to sleep in, certainly not at some lousy hospital. A few days later, I was pitching batting practice before a doubleheader when I accidentally hit our only backup catcher in the leg (it wasn't on purpose, I swear). So then he couldn't bend over, and our manager was asking the shortstop to catch.

I stepped up and said, "Skip, I'll catch. I'm all right."

Well, in the first inning, I took a foul tip to the forehead, and two of my eight stitches popped open. The ump wanted me out of the game, but I ordered our trainer to slap on a Band-aid. "Let's go!" I said. In the fifth inning, I took another ball off the mask. Now, four of the eight stitches were busted. There was blood on my face and on my uniform, and the umpire was getting nauseated. But I finished the game, and I convinced our manager to let me play the second game, too. In the third inning of the second game, one of the opposing players was at the plate, and he got mad at a strike call. He was jawing with the ump and accidentally dropped his bat.

It hit me in the head.

So six of my eight stitches were open, and home plate was a pool of blood. I kept playing.

My two boys, Kelly and Kasey, have carried on my legacy. (By the way, all my kids' names start with the letter *K*—because "K" means strikeout, and I struck out pretty often.) They're tough. When Kelly was in high school, he ripped up his knee returning a punt. He said he heard it tear, but he was thinking, "If Dad were in the stands, there's no way he would want anyone helping me up." I wasn't in the stands. I was managing the Oakland A's at the time. But Kelly said he could hear my voice in his head, saying, "Get up, get up." So he got up, took one step, and collapsed.

He refused to go to a doctor. He said he'd be all right by Monday.

I called him up on the phone. "Got hurt, huh?" I said.

"Yeah," he said.

"You'll be playing next week, huh?"

"I'll try," he said.

Anyway, the knee looked like a watermelon, and his coach was forced to carry him to the hospital because he refused to go on his own. He needed surgery and it took him a full year to rehabilitate it. Doctors said he was lucky to walk again.

But it was just this macho thing we have in our family. We McKeons never get hurt. If you do get hurt, someone will take your place and you'll never get your job back. Ever heard of Wally Pipp?

Kasey—the younger of the two boys—once played football for two weeks with a fractured arm. He played a whole baseball season with bone chips in his elbow. Why? Because Kelly threatened to beat him up if he left the lineup.

When I managed, I didn't like it when my players got hurt. If someone got hit in the wrist with a pitch, I'd run out, spit some of my tobacco juice on his wrist, and rub it in. Tobacco juice was my home-made remedy. It's amazing how many guys shook off their injuries once I started spitting on them.

Yeah, I guess I demanded a lot—from everybody.

When Kelly was younger, I'd always help him with his hitting, but he was too interested in running around with the gals. When I was a kid, I'd hang off tree branches to strengthen my wrists. I'd turn on car headlights so we could play ball at night. But Kelly, he wanted to run with the gals.

Well, I got him back. We had this batting machine at home, and it was standard for Kelly to take 250 swings a day. One night, he was supposed to be getting ready for a date, but I had him take extra work on the machine. His mind was wandering, so I screamed, "You're not paying attention!" I was mad now, and I began pitching to him. He'd always had trouble with inside pitches, so I decided to brush him back. Well, one pitch slipped a little, and I beaned him.

"That'll teach you," I said.

Ah, he was all right. Today, Kelly says he's better off for it. He's doing real well in his company right now, moving up the corporate ladder because he gets off his duff.

My dad was like that, too. In my hometown—South Amboy, New Jersey—my father ran a taxi company, a parking garage, and a towing service. By age 20, he owned a Ford dealership. He was the youngest car dealer in the country. He was hounding me to open a laundromat before laundromats even existed. And he also thought it'd be lucrative for me to open a funeral home.

My dad was also a justice of the peace in South Amboy. People would pass through our town on their way to the Jersey shore driving way too fast. The police would pull them over and bring them to my dad's garage. He'd be under some car, grease all over him. But when the police showed up, he'd calmly stand up, put on his judicial robe, and reach a verdict.

"That'll be 30 bucks or 30 days," he'd say.

The driver would say, "Judge, I ain't got no money."

"Too bad. Lock him up," my dad would say.

So the driver would panic, go out and get some cash from his wife, and pay.

My dad, he was a self-made man who didn't tolerate slackers. Charlie Finley—the former A's owner, who we will talk about later—was sort of the same way. I remember when he signed Dick Allen, who was always begging me for days off. Charlie said, "For goodness sake, Jack. I'll send him a case of Geritol."

And he did.

I liked that.

I was also a member of the South Amboy Special Police. I had important jobs like supervising sledding after big snowstorms.

2
Jack of All Trades
(I Got Around)

WE'RE CALLING THIS book "Jack of All Trades"
because I've done all of the following:

Driven a taxi.

Driven a school bus.

Driven a wrecker.

Pumped gas.

Owned a drive-in restaurant.

Taught school.

Sold tires.

Sold TVs.

Sold refrigerators.

Officiated basketball games.

Delivered mail.

Been a cop.

Worked the night shift in a hosiery mill.

Fixed cars.

Been in the Air Force.

Scouted ballplayers.

Managed ballplayers.

Traded ballplayers.

No, I never opened that funeral home.

You probably think I've got some stories to tell, and you're right.

Back in my taxi days, we got a call late one night, and I told my dad I'd take it. I told him to go to bed. So I picked up some little guy, and he told me to take him to some bar about four miles away. We arrived, and he just walked out of the cab without paying. My dad never would've tolerated that, so I wouldn't either.

I jumped out and said, "Hey buddy, that's two bucks!" I grabbed him, and as he raised his arm to get away, I decked him. He flew across the car. Then he got up and ran inside the bar.

I didn't know what to do, so I went home and went to bed. The next morning, my dad was up bright and early, and I went to join him in the garage. He looked out the window and said, "Hey, here comes Little Freddie." Well, I wasn't looking out the window, and I didn't know who Little Freddie was. Little Freddie walked into the garage. I still hadn't seen him, and my dad said, "Hey, Jack, turn around. I want to introduce you."

I turned around. It was the guy I decked. Little Freddie.

Anyway, my dad went on to say that he'd been dragged out of bed early that morning to bail Freddie out of jail. And now he wanted me to take Freddie downtown. "Jack," he said, "just so you know, Freddie doesn't pay. I send him a bill at the end of every month."

"Oh," I said.

Lucky for me, Freddie had no memory of our encounter the night before. As I drove Freddie downtown that day, he kept rubbing his jaw. He said, "Gosh, I was so drunk last night, I don't remember what happened. I think somebody hit me."

I told him, "Gee whiz, Freddie. When I dropped you off, you were fine."

You know, I didn't mind driving that cab. If I ever had trouble, I'd just go to the police station, where my Uncle Ed was a police captain. One day, for instance, I picked up a passenger at the YMCA, and the guy wanted me to take him to the docks. Usually, the fare anywhere in town was 50 cents, but the roads were pretty rough at the docks, so we usually charged 75 cents to go there. During this particular ride, the guy asked about the fare, and I said, "75 cents." He objected and said he'd only pay 50 cents. I nodded. Instead of driving to the docks, I drove to the police station.

My uncle saw me pull up, walked over, and asked what was wrong.

"This guy doesn't want to pay," I said.

"How much does he owe you?" my uncle asked.

"Well," I said, "it's 75 cents for the cab ride and a buck twenty-five for all of his B.S."

"Well, buddy," my uncle said, "That's two bucks or 30 days."

The guy paid the two bucks, and, in my best umpire's accent, I told him, "OK, pal, outta here!"

The taxicab was the only way I could get around at night. If I wanted to go anywhere, I took the taxi, and that included dates. I went to my prom in my taxi. I picked up my gal and another couple, and we drove down to Asbury Park for the party. A lot of people go to prom in a limo, but I went all decked out in a cab. At least I didn't have to worry about tipping.

Let me introduce you to Walt Nickerson. Back in the late forties, Walt was the only black in South Amboy, and he lived in my dad's garage. He had a cot and a potbelly stove, and he pumped our gas and drove our cabs and so on. Walt was a little guy, about 5′4″. He once drove our baseball team to one of our games in a bus, and the police pulled us over because they couldn't see a driver. That's how short Walt was.

Walt would be off duty on weekends, and he'd go downtown to play the piano in a local bar. He'd park his little car outside, and my buddies and I would push it down the street and hide it. When he'd come outside all drunk, he could never find it.

Anyway, when I was still too young to drive, we got a call to tow a car from a cemetery near our house. Walt drove the wrecker over to get it, and I went with him. We got to the cemetery and discovered that some man had committed suicide in his car. When we saw the body, Walt freaked out. He ran back to the garage on foot and hid. I wasn't even old enough to drive, but I ended up towing the car back myself. We didn't see Walt until the next morning.

Then there was the drive-in restaurant I owned. This was in 1959, when you didn't have too many sports bars around, especially in North Carolina, where I was at the time. We sold beer and soft drinks and hot dogs. Our first night, we grossed exactly 12 bucks.

I decided to take out a newspaper ad, and— bingo—we were grossing 16 bucks a night.

See, this pizza place across the street was killing us. So I went out and bought some frozen pizzas, and we undersold everything—the beer, the hot dogs, the pizza, everything. People began stopping at my place on their way to the beach. Suddenly we were making

200 bucks on Mondays and about 400 bucks on weekends. Unfortunately, we barely broke even because so many people came into the store to rip us off. We'd all be watching TV or something, and some guy would be stealing a case of beer. We ended up selling the joint for $6,000. But hell, we bought it for $900.

And yes, I really did teach school. This was up in New Jersey, where my brother, Biff, was a regular P.E. teacher. When he needed a day off or if he was sick, I'd substitute. The kids loved me, because we just sat around and talked about executing the squeeze play.

I also officiated basketball games. Ah, it kept me in shape, and I didn't exactly take it seriously. If a player would slide on the court, I'd sweep my arms and scream, "Safe!" If a kid knocked another kid over from behind, I'd throw a handkerchief and scream, "Clipping! 15 yards!"

As a ref, though, you gotta be in control. I remember one game when I was working underneath the hoop, and I was supposed to be watching for 3-second violations. Some kid took a shot, and I saw it bound off the rim, so I blew my whistle and said, "No basket, two shots." Well, the ball actually had bounced off the rim and fallen back through the hoop. The scorer's table kept telling me the basket counted, but, hey, I wasn't gonna change my call. I was the ref. I was in control. So I whispered over to the other ref and said, "Did the ball really go in?" He nodded. I coughed and said, "No basket! Someone tipped the ball before it dropped in. That's offensive interference. Two shots!"

Nobody said a word.

Eventually I got to officiate some Atlantic Coast

Conference games. I remember one game between North Carolina and Wake Forest, when the Wake Forest coach, Bones McKinney, kept getting in my face. He said I was letting the North Carolina players push too much. Well, I was one of these refs who let people play. I didn't call ticky-tack fouls. And I knew how to shut coaches up. So after McKinney started yelling at me, I immediately called a foul on one of his players—Lenny Chappel—for pushing. I turned to Bones and said, "Is that what you're talking about?"

He shut up.

Back home in South Amboy, I did just about any job there was to do. I'd fill in from time to time for the regular mailmen. Never got bit by a dog.

As a teenager, I was also a member of the South Amboy Special Police. I had important jobs like supervising sledding after big snowstorms. Kids would sled down these big hills, and I had to make sure no cars got in the way. I got a dollar an hour.

One day, I had to tell this car to get away from the hill, and the driver was some smart-alecky kid. He was giving me lip, but I finally got him outta there. A day later, I was at my regular hangout—the South Amboy Lunch Wagon—and this same smart-alecky kid shows up with three of his friends. I ended up inviting him outside, and I rearranged his ribs.

From that day on, he always waved to me when he saw me.

When the Korean War began I figured I'd join the show. I enlisted in the Air Force and was assigned to Samson Air Force Base in upstate New York. I'd just finished a couple of seasons as a minor leaguer, and two weeks after I got to the base I saw a sign that said "Baseball tryouts." The base had a team. I met a Lt.

Dave Tunno, who saw right away that I'd been a pro ballplayer. First he put me in charge of the ballfield; then he put me in charge of the team.

So, obviously, the Air Force wasn't half bad. Besides running the baseball team, I was in charge of intramural athletics. I had important jobs such as making out schedules for volleyball games and badminton games and handball games and basketball games. I never did see Korea.

I did, however, see Biloxi, Mississippi, when our baseball team reached the East Coast playoffs, and we all flew down for the tournament. Funny thing was, here we were in the Air Force, but it was the first time any of us had been in an airplane. The plane landed with two flat tires, and it scared us to death.

Eventually we flew to San Antonio for the World Air Force Championship. We won, but by then all my guys were petrified of flying. I had to call Dave Tunno to ask if we could take a train home.

And that's what we did. A bunch of guys in the Air Force.

Whatever.

We didn't have any batting coaches back then, so I'd evaluate myself. I'd say, "Jack, change your gosh darn stance." So I copied the stance of Gil McDougald, a former Yankee who used to crouch over like he had a backache. Of course, fans saw me bending over and they'd scream, "Take a nap someplace else, McKeon!" And they'd throw mattresses on the field.

3
I Hit My Weight
(Too Bad I Wasn't
300 Pounds)

ALL KIDDING ASIDE, baseball owes me nothing. I owe baseball something. As a kid, you dream about being a major-league All Star, and you play morning till night. That was me. We used to pull the cars out of my dad's garage and play indoors. We invented the Houston Astrodome before there was an Astrodome.

I didn't have the greatest talent, but I got a lot of help from the people of South Amboy. Allie Clark, who played with the Yankees and Indians, was the first big leaguer ever to come from South Amboy, and he'd take me with him to workouts whenever he could. When he was playing for the Triple-A Newark Bears, I'd tag along with him and catch batting practice. Newark had some guy named Yogi Berra, as well as Bobby Brown, who's now the American League president.

My father tried to come watch me play, but he'd inevitably have to take off on a taxi call. For all he knew, I might have been pretty good.

No, really, I wasn't that bad. The best players in town were the O'Brien brothers—Johnny and Eddie—and me. Johnny and Eddie ended up as All-American basketball players at the University of Seattle, and both played in the big leagues with Pittsburgh.

Pittsburgh signed me, too. But I'm getting ahead of myself.

Growing up, my father helped organize "The McKeon Boys Club." We were all in our teens, and I'd choose the best players around to play against other guys from neighboring towns. Ol' Walt—who needed three pillows to see over the dashboard—would drive our team bus.

I had baseball on the brain. I played for St. Mary's High in the afternoon, then turned my uniform inside out and caught a city league game at 6 P.M. Then, I'd hop a ride over to the town of South River, for a game at 8 P.M. I'd finally get home, eat, and go to bed.

Oops. Forgot to study.

Holy Cross eventually offered me a baseball scholarship, but I wanted to sign a pro contract right out of high school. Scouts from the Pirates and Red Sox were hounding me, but my father thought college was more educational than catching.

I went to Holy Cross, but I was so sad. We had to go to Mass every day, and every day I prayed my dad would let me sign a pro contract. Well, I believe deeply in the Lord, because that's exactly what happened.

Dad let me sign a $215-a-month contract with the Pirates, as long as I agreed to continue my education in the off-season. He still wanted me to be a funeral director.

My first spring training was in New Orleans, 1949. I took the train there, and it was my first time ever in a Pullman car. I stuck my chest out and roamed around the train. I was a ballplayer, man. I played the role.

There were a couple of other players on the train with me, and when we arrived, we didn't know where to go. We didn't know anything about New Orleans, but I remembered listening to the radio all the time as a kid and hearing: "Here's Tommy Dorsey and his band from the Hotel Roosevelt in New Orleans!" So we took a cab to the Hotel Roosevelt.

It wasn't at all what I had in mind. First of all, Tommy Dorsey wasn't there, and everyone was dressed in tuxedos. We had our baseball gear with us, and we were quickly directed to the door.

The doorman told us about another hotel down the road. Tommy Dorsey wasn't there either, but some cockroaches were. We stayed overnight, and finally found our way to the field the next day.

After spring training, I was assigned to a Class D team in Greenville, Alabama. My roommate was Evan Law, brother of the famed pitcher Vern Law. Evan and I were both catchers, but I got all of the playing time. I played literally every day. At one point, I caught 52 straight games; my legs ached and my back ached, and I was sick of squatting. One day, we were playing a doubleheader in the 100-degree Alabama heat, and our team was trailing, 13-1. Poor Evan. He hadn't caught a game in months. And I wanted a breather.

Finally, our manager—Walter Tauchser, formerly of the Dodgers—took me out. I trekked back to take a shower and started jawing "What took him so long! I needed a day off! My leg's killing me!"

One of my teammates stuck his head in the shower and told me to shush up. Tauchser was back there listening to every word I said.

So I wasn't in the lineup the next day.

Or the next day.

So I approached Tauchser and said, "I'm ready to go, Skip."

I caught the next 50 games. And I never, *ever* asked to come out of a game again.

It was pretty easy to stay sober in Greenville. There was no beer in the county, so we had to go 18 miles to Fort Deposit if we wanted a cool one. Actually, the facilities around the whole league were pretty sobering, too. There were railroad tracks right behind the clubhouse in Brewton, Alabama, and trains would shoot by from time to time. The clubhouse would actually shake.

In Andalusia, Alabama, the clubhouse was the size of a dugout. Some guys tried showering there, until they were joined by four snakes. They ended up changing in the bus.

Anyway, we took the pennant that year, winning our final 12 games. I batted .251, which was more than I weighed. When I got to Greenville that spring, I had weighed 235 pounds, but with the heat and all, I got down to 204 pounds by season's end. And people still thought I was fat.

That off-season, I went jogging every day. This was 1950, back when jogging wasn't the trendy thing to do. I'd pile on sweat clothes and go running in 15-degree weather. People in town thought I was a kook, but I reported to spring training weighing 172 pounds.

They still thought I was fat. Big bones, I guess.

My second season, 1950, was my worst. Originally, I was assigned to play for the Class B York Red Roses, but I was the backup catcher, and I didn't like sitting. I asked to be reassigned so I could play. They sent me to Class C ball in Gloversville, New York.

This was the season I got hit in the head with the bat and needed all those stitches. And later, I cracked my ankle sliding into second, and—later—I almost lost my life.

See, I had just broken my ankle, and the team suggested I go home for a while. They told me to go on a Friday, but I told them I'd rather stick around until Sunday. That Friday night, I couldn't sleep at all because my ankle hurt. So I got up at about 4 A.M. and went down to the local coffee shop. I picked up the morning paper and glanced at the front page.

"Munitions Blast in New Jersey Kills 33 People," screamed the headline. But I always start my day by reading the sports page, so that's what I did. Then, out of curiosity, I turned back to the front page to see about that explosion in New Jersey.

It happened in South Amboy.

As it turned out, if I had gone home on Friday, my train would've pulled in to South Amboy approximately two minutes before the explosion. I guess I could've been killed. My Uncle Ed—the police captain—wired me to say everyone was safe at home. The FBI investigated the blast, and they asked my father to go down to the docks and pick up the motors that had exploded. My father loaded them on his wrecker, and good ol' Walt took off like a shot when he saw them back at the garage. We didn't see him for days. He thought they were gonna blow up again.

I ended up hitting .217 that year, which was too darn close to my weight. That's when I enlisted in the Air Force, but I was only in the service a short time. I got a medical discharge because of my bum ankle.

I had made 225 bucks a month the previous season at Class C Gloversville, so I was surprised when Dick Wagner of the Hutchinson (Kansas) Elks (until recently he was the president and general manager of the Houston Astros) offered me a $12.50-a-month raise when I left the service. I'd only hit .217, right? I'd had a lousy year, and I was expecting a pay cut. Today, ballplayers hit .217 and want a $100,000 raise. But not me—I was thankful for the 12 bucks.

Our manager at Hutchinson was Wes Griffin, who really knew how to cheat. He taught our pitchers how to throw spitters, and he taught the rest of us how to sharpen our spikes and break up double plays. You didn't mess with Wes. One night, we were losing, 4-1, and had our fastest runner on third base with one out. Wes was coaching third, and the runner told him, "Skip, I can steal home."

Wes said, "If you go, son, you better keep on going. Because when you start for home plate, I'm starting for the clubhouse to get my new shotgun. So buddy, you better run for cover."

The guy stayed put.

The following year, I was in New Orleans again for spring training, and I got to meet Danny Murtaugh for the first time. Murtaugh, of course, ended up managing the big league Pirates, but back then he had to mess with players like me.

Danny was a great double-talker. I'd be sitting in the dugout and he'd say something like, "Mac, Um ba um ba um ba bullpen?"

The only word I could make out was "bullpen," so I'd ask him, "Danny, you want me to go to the bullpen?"

"No, that's OK," he'd say.

Then he'd say, "Mac, um ba um ba um ba balls?"

I'd say, "Danny, you want me to get the balls?"

"No, that's OK," he'd say. It took me weeks to realize he was double-talking me.

Danny also was a big-time tobacco chewer. You had to be real careful walking by him because he'd spray your pants or your shoes with tobacco juice. He thought it was hilarious.

But Danny saw something in me (maybe it was my inability to hit curve balls). He asked me if I ever thought about managing, and I admitted I had. He said he'd already told Branch Rickey—the Pirate president—that I'd make a good manager.

Well, I spent that 1953 season at Class B Burlington, North Carolina, which is where I became a switch hitter. See, when you're batting .190 and you weigh 220, you're desperate. There was this pitcher in our league—Ramon Monzant, who later pitched for the Giants—who had me figured out. All he did was throw curveballs, and all I did was whiff. Batting right-handed, I just couldn't hit breaking balls. So one day in Winston-Salem, the count got to 2 and 2 against Monzant, and I figured a curveball was coming. I switched over and hit lefty. He missed, and the count was 3 and 2. I figured he'd throw a fastball now, so I switched back to the right side. Jimmy Brown, the Winston-Salem manager who had been the second baseman for the old St. Louis Gashouse Gang, started howling. "Put him in a cage! Put him in a cage!"

I'll never forget my first lefty home run. We were in Danville, Virginia, for a playoff game, and one of our slowest runners was on first base with one out. Funny, I was always a better hitter with men on base. With nobody on, I never concentrated. Well, with a slow runner on first, I tugged at my sleeve. That meant the hit-and-run was on. All I wanted to do was make contact. That's all I wanted.

Well, I accidentally hit it over the fence.

The third-base coach passed out.

At that point in my career, all I ever wanted to do was hit the darn ball. We didn't have any batting coaches back then, so I'd evaluate myself. I'd say, "Jack, change your gosh darn stance." So I copied the stance of Gil McDougald, a former Yankee who used to crouch over like he had a backache. Remember Eddie Gaedel, the midget of St. Louis? It was sort of like that stance, too—all hunched over. Like Rickey Henderson today, but much more exaggerated.

The first time I used it, I homered to win a game in the 14th inning. I was hooked. Of course, I never heard the end of it. Fans saw me bending over and they'd scream, "Take a nap someplace else, McKeon!" And they'd throw mattresses on the field.

In one game, we had a man on third base, and I was in my crouch at the plate. The pitcher threw a fat one down the middle, and I was gonna swing for the fences. But the catcher tipped my bat, and I couldn't make contact. I turned to the ump, Art Talley, and yelped, "Let me tell you something. If he tips my bat again, all hell's gonna break loose. You understand?"

I got back in the box, and the catcher tipped my bat again on the next pitch. I didn't say a word, I didn't do a thing.

I just got back in the box. But instead of striding toward the ball on the next pitch, I strode toward the catcher, and got him right on the mask. He went down, the ball hit the umpire on the chest protector and our runner scored from third.

So the catcher and I got in the darndest fight right there at home plate. I whipped him pretty good, and we both got thrown out of the game.

I showered and shaved. I went to the stands to watch the rest of the game. I saw this beautiful gal sitting near me, and I drummed up a conversation.

"Oh, you're that rowdy," she said.

She didn't want much to do with me at first, but I'd always see her walking downtown during her lunch break. Carol was her name, and she still thought I was a rowdy. I kept after her, though, and we eventually got together.

We eventually got married.

I was enjoying my days in Burlington. A bunch of us lived in Graham, which was only a couple miles away from our ballpark. We didn't have cars or bicycles, so we used to hitchhike to the park. People would gladly pick us up, and they'd inevitably ask us what we did for a living. Well, my old manager, Wes Griffin, had advised me never to say you were a ballplayer. You'd get bugged to death. So we began telling people we were soil experts or we were going to work on refrigerated tankers, that sort of thing. One day, we told a guy we were Christian Science Workers. He said, "Oh! I believe in the Lord, too!" We told him we'd just been to North Carolina State University to save a brother who'd gone astray. And now we were on our way to Elon College to save another brother. I was in the front seat, and I had to look directly out the window so this guy wouldn't see me laughing. Finally, he let us out and screamed, "I believe in the Lord! I believe in the Lord! Please pray for me!"

Living outside Burlington wasn't always such a treat. Our manager—Stan Wentzel, formerly of the

Boston Braves—would order 9 A.M. workouts if we lost a few games in a row. Well, by the time a night game ended, it was late. And by the time we'd eaten, it was 2 A.M. So we'd never go home at all. We'd run over to the trainer's house, throw pebbles at his window, wake him up, and ask for the clubhouse key. Then we'd run over to the stadium and sleep in the locker room. One night we decided to sleep on the field instead. A couple guys were using second base for a pillow, a couple others were using first base, and I was over sleeping on third.

Wentzel would show up about 8 A.M., and he'd say, "These guys really want to play ball!"

The '53 season ended, and I decided to stick around Burlington—Carol was there. I had met Doc Mathis, the athletic director at Elon College, and he asked me if I'd help him coach basketball and baseball. In exchange, I'd be given free school tuition. I'd been going to school at Seton Hall in New Jersey, but I transferred to Elon.

I was going to school from 8 o'clock till noon, officiating basketball games from 6 to 11, and working the third shift in a hosiery mill from midnight to 7. I picked up about 70 bucks a week officiating, and I got about 35 bucks working at the hosiery mill. Needed some Geritol.

I went back to Burlington for the 1954 baseball season and got a call from Branch Rickey, who'd remembered I wanted to be a manager. Remember? Danny Murtaugh had told him.

Anyway, Rickey offered me a managing job in Clinton, Iowa. I told him, "Great!" I told him I was gonna quit school and take the job, but he said, "You're in school? No, no, no. I'm not gonna keep you from a college education."

So I stayed put. But I dreamed more and more about managing. I was second-string at Burlington, and I saw all these great catchers coming up—Roy Campanella and Yogi Berra and Joe Garagiola. My goal was to reach the big leagues, but I figured I probably wouldn't make it. At least not as a player.

Finally, Branch Rickey called me back one day. I wasn't around to take the call, but Red Fowler, the Burlington owner, told me Rickey wanted me to do him a favor and play in Hutchinson, Kansas. Goodness gracious, I was about to get married, we were in first place, and I just didn't want to go. But it was Branch Rickey, so I had Fowler call him back and say yes.

Rickey told Fowler, "Good. I just wanted to see if he'd do me a favor. Tell him he's going out there to manage."

So out I went. I met the team in Ponca City, Oklahoma, but I was told I wouldn't take over as manager for a week or so. Instead, they put me behind the plate.

One morning, I picked up the paper and saw a headline that made my head spin: "Larry Dorton named Hutchinson manager."

Wow, I thought *I* was the new Hutchinson manager.

I called the Hutchinson GM—Dick Wagner—and Wagner called Rickey. There'd been a mix-up. Rickey never told his farm director about me, and the farm director hired somebody else for the job, but Rickey guaranteed I'd manage the team the next season.

The league folded over the winter.

So back to North Carolina I went. I was in school at Elon when the Fayetteville club called and needed me to catch for them. I was batting .285 (way over my weight), my best start ever. But Fayetteville had to release me because we were only allowed 15 veterans, and I was the 16th. The owner asked me, "You want to manage, don't you?"

I nodded, but by this time I was thinking about that funeral home.

"Well, don't do anything for two weeks," he said. "We might want you."

In the meantime, the Greensboro Red Sox wanted me to catch for them, which I agreed to do as long as they gave me my release if Fayetteville came through with the managing job. Unfortunately, our first game was against Fayetteville, and when the Fayetteville owner saw me he screamed, "I told you not to do anything for two weeks!"

When I finally calmed him down, he hired me as his player-manager.

What a team. Only two players were younger than me. My best pitcher was a construction worker who only showed up on days he pitched. My ace relief pitcher worked at Western Electric and wouldn't show up until the fifth inning. Another guy was a high school football coach and couldn't show up until football practice ended. At times, we had only 11 guys in uniform.

One night my second baseman, Bobby Lyons, got beaned in the head with a fastball. His life was in danger, and it was my job to keep him awake in the ambulance. I told him a joke or two, and we finally got to the hospital.

Well, they couldn't reach Bobby's wife or our club president. The hospital needed consent to operate, and it was all in my hands. They said he could be dead in 12 hours without surgery. I whispered the situation to Bobby, who was semiconscious. With surgery, there was 50–50 chance that he'd live.

"That's a .500 average, Skip," he said. "I'll take it."

As they wheeled him in, he said faintly, "Pray for me Jack."

I was crying. This was managing?

Bobby made it through, but he certainly wasn't ready to play for a while. The Fayetteville club waived him rather than pay his salary. Do you believe that? I was livid. On top of that, when I hurt my hand and doctors ordered me to rest 10 days, the Fayetteville owner said, "You don't play, we don't pay."

They released me, too.

I went back to school and was taking exams when I received an urgent message from a guy named Nick Mariana in Missoula, Montana. He had heard my name from Branch Rickey. His telegram said, "Need hustling young manager. Are you available?"

I was out the door.

I eventually finished my playing career a few years later in 1959. I was a player-manager at the time, and on this particular night I was catching Lee Stange, who eventually pitched for the Twins and Red Sox. The fans were all over me because they thought I should be playing young kids. I was 27, so I guess that was old. Hell, our third baseman, Carlos "Potato" Pascual, was 32, but, of course, he was leading the league in hitting.

I might've led the league in passed balls.

Well, on this particular night I just couldn't handle Stange's curve ball. One of his pitches broke and hit the plate and bounced over my head. The runners moved up. The same thing happened on the very next pitch and two runs came in. The next day, I saw the two passed balls charged to me in the box score and said, "That's it."

I don't usually quit, I know. I'm Mr. Geritol, I know.

But it was time to go.

My personal MVP was Joe Abernathy, a pitcher. He knew how to drive the bus.

4
I Managed
(To Make a Living)

I GUESS 600 bucks a month is a living. That's how much money I made in Missoula, Montana, at my first real managing job. Nick Mariana had just purchased the Odgen club of the Pioneer League and decided to move it to *Missoula* of all places. He named the team the Timberjacks. Problem was, he had no players and no place for spring training.

He put me in charge. I took a road trip south and begged, borrowed, and stole players from independent clubs in Georgia and Florida. I got myself a bunch of Cubans. We trained in the mountains of North Carolina, and I broke camp with 17 players. Not necessarily *good* players, but there were 17 of them, that's for sure.

My personal MVP was Joe Abernathy, a pitcher. He knew how to drive the bus.

Missoula welcomed us with open arms. They'd never had a team before, and I'm not sure they knew much about the game at all. They cheered every ball that was hit hard, fair or foul.

The whole town chipped in to give us gifts. Each game, the first player to single got a case of Coca-Cola and the first player to walk got a banana split. Same thing for the first home run, the first double, the first triple, and so on. One of the diners in town gave out free ham and eggs to the first double-play combination. So whenever a runner got on base, our infield would chirp, "Ham and eggs . . . Ham and eggs . . . Ham and eggs."

Most of the guys chewed tobacco, including me, so I convinced a local storeowner to give the team a six-pack of chew after the first error. Whenever we'd get a little low on chew, I'm not saying we booted any ground balls on purpose, but—uh—errors *are* part of the game.

I put myself behind the plate from time to time, but that turned out to be dangerous. There was a trap door to the right of home plate, the only way to get in and out of our clubhouse. Well, I sent one of my pitchers to the showers one day, and he forgot to close the trap door. The next batter popped a fly behind the plate, and I fell down the trap door trying to catch it.

One of my players joked, "Hey, Skip! That catch was out of sight." Thanks.

Bob Uecker played in that league, too. He wasn't a bad catcher, and I considered him a big-league prospect. And he made it, despite what you hear.

After Missoula, I managed in such places as Appleton, Wilson, Vancouver, Dallas-Fort Worth, Atlanta, and High Point. There are at least a million or two or three stories I could tell about managing in the bush leagues, but I think you'll have to settle for just a few.

We once lost six in a row in Missoula, and people began staying away from the ballpark. So we decided to have a "Break The Jinx Night." Here was the plan: First, I went and found a blank gun at a local store. Then I grabbed this little kid named Smokey who was always hanging around selling newspapers. Smokey, he was gonna be the jinx. We dressed him up in a black cape and mask, and he showed up on the right-field fence about 15 minutes before the first pitch. I had the PA announcer scream, "Hey, there's the Jinx!"

Suddenly, the players charged out onto the field and started to chase him. One of them had the blank gun, to shoot him. Smokey played dead.

We had borrowed a hearse and a casket from a local funeral home, and six of the players dressed as pallbearers. We stuck Smokey inside the casket, had a little ceremony, and drove him away.

The we went out and lost our seventh straight.

It was right around that time that I was mistaken for a bank robber. After every game, owner Nick Mariana had me deposit the gate receipts at the Montana National Bank. I had keys to make the deposits late at night. Well, I turned the key one night and the burglar alarm went on. Before I knew it, two cops had me pinned against the wall. They took the money and frisked me and threatened to take me downtown. They didn't believe me until I finally reached the bank president, who came downtown, checked out the bank, and decided everything was in order. I mean, I couldn't steal when I was on base; I sure wasn't going to try in a bank.

What really made it all worthwhile were the kids who went on to greater things. In 1959, I was managing the Twins' farm team in Appleton, Wisconsin, and I had a 17-year-old shortstop named Zoilo Ver-

salles, who was the American League MVP in 1965.
Zoilo was a Cuban kid who didn't know much En-
glish at first. We were in Topeka when he got called
up to the big leagues. He was supposed to meet the
Twins in Chicago. Hell, there were no direct flights
from Topeka to Chicago, so I arranged for Zoilo to
take the train to Kansas City and then fly from KC to
Chicago. But when I gave Zoilo his itinerary, he just
kept saying, "No comprendo, Skip. No comprendo."

Finally, I pinned three messages on his sport coat.
The first said, "Train conductor: Let me off in Kansas City." The second one said, "Direct me to a cabbie and have him take me to the Kansas City airport." And the third one said, "Direct me to the
Chicago flight." I told him to point to his coat when
he got in trouble.

"Si," he said. "Si."

I guess he made it.

One more thing about Zoilo. He was once playing
shortstop for me in a game at Sioux City, Iowa. It was
freezing out, there was no score, and they had a man
on second base in the seventh inning. Someone hit a
grounder to Zoilo, and he threw it way over the first
baseman's head.

I wouldn't have minded, but I looked closer and
saw that Zoilo was wearing fur gloves.

I flipped. I told him, "Get the hell out of here!" Of
course, he didn't mind because he headed straight
into the warm clubhouse. So I dragged him back
out. I told him, "If we have to freeze, you're gonna
freeze with us!"

Oh, you see 'em all. I had a pitcher named Jim
Schrode, who, for some reason, decided one night
to wear his sunglasses. We were playing a twi-night
doubleheader, and he started the second game. When
he went to warm up, he took his shades with him.

I ran out to the mound. "You cracking up or something, Jimmy?" I asked.

"No, Skip," he said. "I just need to wear my sunglasses."

Oh. Right.

So I left him alone, hoping no one would notice. No one said anything, but in the second inning when it started snowing, I think he got some funny looks.

But that was pretty mild compared to the Moon Child. I've heard a lot of excuses from players, but outfielder John Wyatt outdid 'em all. One night, he blew an easy pop-up. Claimed he lost it in the moon.

We called him "Moonbeams" from then on.

Mind you, I wasn't always amused by these guys. In Appleton, I had Carlos "Potato" Pascual as my third baseman. He was probably the best player on the team, but I didn't play favorites.

We were going to Burlington, Iowa, and our team bus was scheduled to leave at 12:30 P.M. On the button. At 12:25, we were all on the bus, except Potato, and I told the bus driver to start the motor. Bob Willis, our general manager, ran up and shouted, "You can't leave! You can't leave! Potato's not here!"

I told Willis the bus left at 12:30, no exceptions. As we pulled away, Willis was pounding on the door: "Don't leave! Don't leave!"

I didn't care what Potato's batting average was. We left, and Willis ended up flying Potato in. I wouldn't play him. Rules are rules.

I could probably fill a book with bus stories. We used to drive over this long, dangerous bridge in Dubuque, Iowa—we'd come down a real steep hill, full speed ahead, and then we'd hit the bridge. It made the guys a little queasy, especially our Cuban players.

One night, I suggested that our bus driver—

Wally—drive over the bridge blindfolded. The Cubans went crazy, "No, no. You can't do that, Skip. You just can't."

I told them Wally knew that road so well, it'd be no problem. So, at about 4 A.M., we were heading toward the bridge. I put a handkerchief halfway over Wally's eyes.

"Can you see?" I asked him.

"Sure can," he said.

Then I woke up the Cubans. "Look, Look!" I said. "Wally's driving over the bridge blindfolded! He can't see!"

The Cubans crawled under their seats. They were in a rage: "You crazy, mahn. You crazy, mahn. We see GM tomorrow. We no ride with you no more."

I guess the GM calmed them down, because they were back on the bus the next day. Although they did stop breathing for a few seconds when we crossed that bridge.

One night, coming from Lincoln, Nebraska, we stopped at a diner in Davenport, Iowa. I grabbed a burger and walked up to pay my bill. Well, the guy in front of me was loaded, absolutely drunk. The cashier lady told him he owed $10.95, and he gave her a twenty. As she was counting his change, I disguised my voice and said, "Keep the change."

The lady said, "Oh thank you, sir." Meanwhile, the drunk didn't catch on: "Hey, where's my money! What kind of place is this." And he stumbled out.

Another night, we were on our way home to Appleton very late when we stopped at a diner in Columbus, Wisconsin. The joint had just opened at 5 A.M., and we showed up at 5:10. All 20 of us piled out of the bus.

There was one guy on duty. He'd take one order, cook the meal, and come back to take the next order.

He did this one by one, and he wasn't exactly doing it in world record time. Every time he walked by me, I'd say, "Got any coffee?"

"It's coming," he'd say.

Well, he kept bringing the guys burnt toast and dry eggs, one by one, and I kept agitating him.

"Got any coffee?"

"It's coming."

"Got any coffee?"

"It's coming."

Then I said, "Got any burnt toast?"

That did it. He called us troublemakers and said I was the biggest troublemaker of all. Only six of us ended up getting served—I never did get my coffee—so we walked out without paying.

Well, we felt pretty bad and came back to slip him a twenty. But his door was locked. And now the cops were there. We explained the whole deal to them, and they told us not to worry. Apparently the guy was always calling the cops on his customers. They told us to beat it.

Anyway, every time we drove through Columbus, Wisconsin, we'd stop in front of his diner and honk our horn.

He'd lock his door.

Oh, I had a great time with the Cubans. In Missoula, the Twins gave me a little Cuban named Sandy Valdespino, who was supposedly very fast. In his first game, the score was tied in the ninth inning, and he led off with a triple. I was coaching third, and Jay Ward—later the hitting coach for the Yankees—was up to bat. I told Sandy, "Wait for the ball to go through the infield before you run. Comprende? Wait for the ball to go through."

"Si," he said.

Ward, on the first pitch, chopped a one-hopper

down to third. I looked up and Sandy was gone. He was out by a mile, and we lost the game in 10 innings.

The next night, we were in another tie game in the ninth when he led off with a single. Great. I was gonna sacrifice him to second. Benny Sinquefield, my number 2 hitter, put down a perfect bunt, and the pitcher had no choice but to throw to first. But wait! Sandy didn't stop at second—he was going for third. He was out by 15 feet, as I covered my eyes.

I told him, "This is not Cuba-style baseball! This is America!" But he wasn't even listening.

I was gonna get him. I went down to a hardware store and bought a clothesline. The next time Sandy got on, I was gonna have my first base coach—Gene Curtis—lasso him.

Sure enough, Sandy walked, and I sent a batboy out with the clothesline. Curtis tied it around Sandy, whose eyeballs got so big I thought they were gonna pop out. I had the next hitter take the first two pitches. Sandy's eyeballs were getting bigger. When we finally took the clothesline off of him, we never had a problem again.

Let me tell you another story about Sandy. His roommate at Missoula was pitcher Jim Kaat, who ended up spending 25 years in the big leagues. Jim was about 6'5"; Sandy was about 5'8". Mutt 'n' Jeff. Wherever Jimmy went, Sandy followed. Whatever Jimmy did, Sandy did. Whatever Jimmy ordered at a restaurant, Sandy ordered. Their favorite meal was ham and eggs (not because they were a double-play combination). They'd be walking down the street and we'd say, "There's ham and there's egg."

Oh, we had a blast in Vancouver. I bought some big index cards for the Cubans. I wrote, "hit and run" and "bunt" and "steal" in Spanish on the cards and took them with me to third base. That's how I'd flash the signs. If they couldn't understand that, I told them, they were history.

It worked.

But they were great kids and great workers. And I guess I shouldn't have given them such a hard time, because they sure weren't the only guys to screw up on the basepaths.

In Wilson, North Carolina, I had another Cuban, Juan Visteur. Juan was a pretty good centerfielder, but he must have had too much wax in his ears. He'd be rounding third, and I'd hold him up, hollering, "Whoa, whoa."

He'd run by and be out by 20 feet. This would happen about every other day. One day, I said, "You do it again, and I'll shoot your ass!"

A little later, I'm walking down the street in Greensboro, and I see a store sign: "Blank Guns For Sale." I bought two.

I stuck the guns in my back pocket and waited.

About two weeks later, Juan was on second and one of my guys hit a ball up the middle. It looked like it might make it through to center field, but the second baseman dove and knocked it down. I held Juan up. I put my arms way over my head, screaming, "Whoa, whoa." He zoomed by me.

I had no choice but to shoot his ass. I reached for my guns and unloaded: Pow! Pow! Pow! I fired about seven shots. Juan, about 30 feet from home plate, did the darndest swan dive you've ever seen. The throw from second was wild, and he was safe. But he wouldn't get up. His hands were covering his head. He thought his ass was shot.

Never had a problem with him again.

Listen, I liked him. Later, we were playing Burlington and I waved him in to score. He slid in safe, the throw coming way too late. But the Burlington catcher—Doc Edwards, who became manager of the Cleveland Indians in 1987—jumped right on top of Juan and knocked the wind out of him.

I ran down from the coaching box, put my finger in Doc's face, and said, "That was uncalled for. The play was over. I oughta knock you on your ass—and I think I will!"

So, I decked him with a right cross, and we had an all-out brawl right there at home plate.

The next week, we were playing Burlington again, this time at their stadium. I called Brodie Hood, their general manager, and said, "Let's have some fun. Let's put up a boxing ring in front of the pitcher's mound, and I'll fight your manager, Pinkie May. It won't be real, but we'll pack 'em in."

Well, Brodie decided against it. But when we got into town, the newspapers named me "Ingemar McKeon" after Ingemar Johansson, the former heavyweight boxer.

Hey, if a guy is terrorizing one of your players, you've gotta do something about it.

One night when I was coaching third base in Winston-Salem, we'd hit back-to-back homers, and their pitcher started brushing back some of our hitters. I hollered at the pitcher, "You classless jerk," or something to that effect. Not what you'd say to your best buddy, but I've heard worse.

Well, their third baseman—I forget the idiot's name—turned to me and said, "Why don't you give it a rest."

"Shut your mouth, pal, and stay out of it," I said, "or I'll deck you."

"You don't have the guts," he snapped.

Well, just as he said that, my batter grounded a ball up the middle. Everyone was watching the play, but I jumped the third baseman and started beating the hell out of him.

Listen, you can't have a pitcher throwing at your players. Pitchers are a whole different breed. You never know what's coming next. When I was in Wilson, about 1961, the Twins sent us a phenom pitcher named Jimmy Roland. They'd just drafted him out of high school and signed him to a $50,000 bonus—an all-time record for the Twins at the time. I figured I'd bring him along slowly. He started one night in Winston-Salem, and he was remarkable. He was striking guys out left and right, and he had a no-hitter going in the seventh.

Then he walked one guy. Then another. And then he was squirming around out there, like he had ants in his pants. He was making some serious gyrations.

I rushed out and said, "What's wrong with you?"

"Skip," he said, "I gotta go to the bathroom."

"Right here?" I asked. "Right here in the middle of your no-hitter?"

The clubhouse wasn't even close to the ballfield, and the dugout didn't have a toilet like most major league dugouts do. He said he'd try to hold it in and get out of the inning.

Well, he made it, but he was the second batter that next inning, and there was no time to get to the clubhouse. Maybe after his at-bat, he'd have time.

But, you guessed it, he singled and he stayed on base until the inning ended. So he had no choice but to get back on the mound. Somebody got a hit off him, and then he walked somebody else. He was squirming again, gritting his teeth and rolling his eyeballs.

I rushed out and said, "Again?"

He was desperate. "Skip, I gotta go. I gotta go. That's it."

He flipped me the ball, and that was the end of the one-hitter.

One more story about Jimmy: In another game, he had a two-hitter and a 2–1 lead in the sixth inning with a man on first base (before the game, I'd made sure he'd been to the john). The next batter put down a perfect sacrifice bunt toward Jimmy, who tripped over the ball and fell down. He lay there, holding his leg.

I rushed out. I mean, this was the Twins' bonus baby.

"Is it your knee?" I asked.

"Yeah," he said.

Then I touched his ankle. "Or is it your ankle?"

"Yeah," he said.

We rushed him to the hospital. They took x-rays, and Jimmy sat there in a wheelchair, totally demoralized.

"They say my ankle's broke, Skip," he said.

Well, I knew Jimmy had also broken his ankle in high school, so I told the doctor about it. He said, "Hmmmmm."

He went back and looked at the x-rays again and said, "You know, it didn't really look like a fresh break. I think what we saw in the x-rays was the old injury." So they taped Jimmy up, and I said, "Let's go. The doctor says the break was your old injury."

"Oh," Jimmy said. And he hopped up and walked swiftly out of the hospital.

The next day, he was even running with the rest of the pitchers in the outfield. I had to pull him aside and say, "Hell, Jimmy. Don't run with those guys, not after that exhibition you put on here in the stadium yesterday. Everyone thought you were dead. For chrissake, limp a little at least."

So he limped.

Well, we'd won the 1961 Carolina League pennant, and Joe Haynes, the Twins' executive vice-president, gave me the choice of being a big-league coach in Minnesota or a Triple-A manager in Vancouver. I was 30 and I really wanted to manage. So I became a Vancouver Mountie.

My coach was George Bamberger, who went on to manage the Mets and the Brewers. I had never met Bambi, and since he was five years older than me I was worried that there might be some resentment on his part. I thought he might try to turn my players against me.

But Bambi was a peach, one of the greatest men I've ever met. We got into a lot of mischief together.

One time in Spokane, we were ahead, 2–1, and they had runners on second and third with the pitcher at the plate. I knew the opposing manager— Preston Gomez—was gonna try the squeeze play. I just knew. I looked over to my catcher and called a pitch-out. So naturally, my pitcher threw it right down the middle. The batter bunted, and the run scored from third on the squeeze. The game was tied.

Now there was a guy on third and still one out. I brought in a new pitcher and told him to throw four straight pitch-outs. I knew Preston was gonna squeeze again. I told my catcher, too, and he said, "Gotcha, Skip."

So what happens? My pitcher throws a curve for a strike. I'm going crazy. Then, he throws another curve, and they bunt in another run. We lose.

Afterward, I'm going bonkers. I'm talking to a

couple of sportswriters, and I say, "You guys know any electronics people in town? I want to wire my pitchers and catchers so I can tell them what the hell to do!"

Both writers laughed, but one of them wanted to know if I was serious. I was. I'd been thinking about it a couple years.

Well, this writer had a couple friends in town who worked for an electronics firm, and he brought them to the ballpark. They said they could wire the pitcher, but not the catcher: a catcher would have too much gear on his body. But with a pitcher, we could just slip a receiver inside his shirt pocket.

Within a week, they had the transmitter and receiver all ready. We needed to test it first, and we had to do it in secret because I'd promised the writer he'd get the exclusive story when we used it in a game. Late one night, Bambi, my trainer Buck Chamberlain, my scout Dick Hager, and I went to test it on a hill near the ballpark. They'd flash their flashlights if they heard me. And they did hear me. It worked, a good 200 feet away. A pitcher was sure to hear me from the dugout.

The next night we had a doubleheader scheduled and I was gonna have Bambi pitch the second game. He'd be my guinea pig. In between games I had planned on letting the rest of the players know about it, but some scout came to visit my office, and I couldn't get rid of him. By the time I did, the players were already back out on the field.

So Bambi was on his own. I walked out to the dugout with what looked like a doctor's bag; I had all my electronic gear inside. I pulled out my transmitter and raised the antenna. I started talking to Bambi. My players thought I was talking to myself.

Every inning or so, I'd let a few players in on the secret, but I never got a chance to tell my first baseman, Ray Looney, and that was unfortunate. See, I could tell Bambi how big a lead a runner was taking off first. Bambi wouldn't even have to look. I could just say, "Throw!" and he'd throw.

I couldn't resist. This one guy was taking a huge lead off first, and I screamed, "Throw!" Bambi wheeled, threw, and hit Ray in the chest.

Fortunately, the shortstop knew what was going on. I told him to break for second base whenever he thought he could pick a guy off. I'd say, "Throw!" and Bambi was picking guys off left and right.

It was a hell of a debut. The headlines screamed: "Vancouver Mounties Make Baseball History." The next day, the Canadian National Network sent a broadcast crew down, and we were besieged. That night, I wired pitcher Jerry Arrigo, who later pitched for the Twins, Reds, and White Sox. Arrigo had been inconsistent, and by wiring him I felt I could work on his pitch selection and things like that, not to mention pickoffs.

But in the third inning, someone told me our signal could be heard on the radio. And then we saw the opposing team listening to it. So we started coding our instructions. Green meant curveball, blue meant fastball, and so on.

The next day, I got a call from the Canadian communication bureau. They wanted me to send my equipment to Ottawa to see if I'd infringed someone's patent. In the meantime, I couldn't use it in Canada. But I could in the United States.

We arrived for a game in Spokane, and newspapers were calling us "The Electronic Mounties." I thought this was a dynamite way to attract fans, so I called the Spokane club president, Spencer Harris, who was always asking me for promotion ideas. I told Spencer to get some radar equipment to place on top of his dugout, so it'd look like he was intercepting our signal. He loved the idea. They ended up with a miniature radar screen on top of the dugout and a guy sitting at a table with headphones on. Hell, I thought they might actually be intercepting us. Jerry Arrigo was pitching again, and just to make sure nothing funny was going on, I even asked him if he wanted to hear some music while he was warming up. I turned on the Red Robbins Rock 'N Roll Show, figuring if Spokane was picking up our signal, they'd start laughing or something when they heard the music. No reaction.

Then I tried, "Cab No. 99, Cab No. 99. Pick up a lady at the Davenport Hotel. Over and out." No reaction. We were safe.

As we toured the west coast, people dubbed us "The Wireless Kids" and "The Space Cadets." I took an old cracked helmet and painted our own call letters on it. I bought an antenna at an auto-parts store and attached it to the helmet. I wore it in the third-base coaching box.

Once in San Diego, Bambi pitched and got knocked out in the fourth inning. As we were walking off, some fan shouted, "Hey, Bamberger! You were tuned in to the wrong station!"

Another time, we decided to have some fun with the Hawaii player, Charlie White, a former catcher with the Orioles. Before the game, Bambi wore the receiver in his shirt pocket and walked over toward White. They began chatting while I was in the other dugout. All of a sudden, I shouted into the transmitter, "Charlie, lose some weight."

Charlie looked around and had no idea. Then I

said it again. I don't think he ever figured it out.

Once, the transmitter really got me out of a jam. In 1962, the Twins' Triple-A affiliate was Dallas-Fort Worth, so that's where I was sent. We played half our games in Dallas and half our games in Fort Worth. On Sundays, we'd play doubleheaders—the first game in Dallas, the second game in Fort Worth.

One day, we were killing Oklahoma City, 16–2. The Okie City manager, Grady Hatton, had been thrown out, as had six of his players. They were all upset at umpire Russ Goetz, who later made it to the American League. Hatton had actually thrown a shin guard at Goetz.

Late in the game, the Oklahoma City pitcher was still griping at Goetz. Goetz just stood there and took it all. But then, when one of my players argued about a strike call, Goetz told him to shut up.

That did it. I ran out and really raised hell. Why get all over my guy? We'd been good sports all afternoon. I got ejected. Afterward, one of the sportswriters went to ask Goetz about the rhubarb, and the writer said Goetz's shirt was polka-dotted with tobacco juice. My tobacco juice.

Well, Hatton got suspended for throwing the shin guard at Goetz, and when Hatton read in the paper that I'd supposedly spit on Goetz, he said I should've been suspended, too. And the league president agreed with him.

Hell, I didn't spit on purpose.

But I didn't worry about it. I sat in the stands and used my transmitter to tell Bambi what to do in the dugout. Goetz saw me in the stands, but he thought I was talking to myself.

Boy, in those days, we did anything for publicity. In Vancouver in 1962, Dick Hager (who now scouts for the Padres) signed a kid named Jim Cowan for the Twins. Cowan wasn't an extra special kid, but he had a good arm, and Dick liked him. Actually, Dick found out about the kid from his birddog scout. A birddog scout is someone who scouts a certain area of the country and tries to sniff out all the prospects. Anyway, I was in Vancouver with Dick, and I got an idea. All we needed was a real live birddog and a photographer. We'd snap a picture of this dog pointing at this kid, Cowan. Then we'd sent the photo to a bunch of newspapers, with the caption, "Birddog spots player."

We actually found a dog who knew how to point.

Hell, it made it in a bunch of papers.

We used to play Denver, and Mile High Stadium had a heck of an exploding scoreboard. Anytime a Denver player homered, there was a minute-long fireworks show. It's great if you're a Denver fan, but obnoxious if you've given up the home run.

So I fixed that. I brought my two blank guns to the ballpark one day, and I put on my own show when we homered. If we could homer. Denver hit two home runs early in the game, and I had to listen to those damn fireworks. But we finally hit one, and I whipped out my guns and started firing away. The crowd thought it was funny, so I loaded up and did it again on our next home run. It got to be a regular thing when Dallas-Fort Worth came to town.

Of course, there are worse things than an exploding scoreboard. An exploding manager, for example.

We developed a great rivalry with the Denver club, mainly because we usually beat them. At one point, we'd beat them 20 of 21 games, and there was a lot of tension on their part whenever we met. Well, on the last night of our season series, I brought out the lineup card, and Denver's coach, Red Ruffing (the former Yankee great), said, "Let's not have any fights tonight."

I said, "Don't worry. Why would we fight you? We always win."

But we were getting beat, 5–4, in the bottom of the ninth, with two guys on. One of my outfielders, Lee Green, was up, and I ordered him to bunt. He fouled off two balls. One more foul bunt, and he was out. Well, he squared around again, but the pitch was way inside. Green fell backward to get out of the way, but the ball inadvertently hit his bat and rolled foul. The umpire called strike three.

I came rushing out, screaming, "No way! No way! He wasn't bunting! He was just getting out of the way!" Meanwhile, the Denver pitcher told the ump, "Don't listen to him. You called it right."

I glared at the pitcher and said, "Get your ass back on the mound."

"Make me," he said.

And as soon as he said, "Make me," I made him. We fought like hell. Guys from their team were piling on top of me, but I had his hair in my hands. Every time someone jumped on me, I'd accidentally smash his head on the ground.

Accidentally.

Of course, when you're a reasonably big guy, you don't worry about getting into fights. But it's hell for smaller guys. Our clubhouse boy in Dallas-Forth Worth was a puny kid named Wayne Hathaway. You couldn't help but pick on the guy. Maybe you know the type. After most games, the players would sit around the clubhouse and drink a few beers. Instead of throwing the cans in the trash, they'd throw 'em at Wayne.

He came into my office complaining. He threatened to quit. I said, "Now, now, Wayne. I'll hold a team meeting and straighten this out."

I wasn't really serious. I mean, what was I gonna say? So I decided to hold a team meeting, but it was just gonna be for show. With Wayne watching, I told the players, "God damnit, Wayne is the best clubhouse guy in baseball! Leave him alone! If I see you mistreating him, I'll ship you outta here."

Wayne was all smiles, so I left the room. But when Wayne walked near the players, they all threw empty soda cans at him.

If that wasn't enough, Wayne had to deal with Dino Williams. Dino was our biggest player, and also Wayne's biggest agitator. Wayne weighed 98 pounds soaking wet, and Dino used to pick him up and spin him around 20 times in the air. When he finally put Wayne down, Wayne—all dizzy—would fall flat on his face.

So I did Wayne a favor and got a wrestler friend of mine to show him some moves. Then I had an even better idea. I scheduled a wrestling match between Wayne and Big Dino. We'd hold it before one of our games, right in front of the mound. We billed Dino as "The Country Boy!" He came out riding a donkey, wearing overalls. Wayne, meanwhile, was escorted out by two beauty queens.

Dino played along. He took a few phony falls. Then he started getting a little steamed at Wayne, and threw him out of the ring. That was that.

Sometimes when things get tense, you have to find a way to ease up. My last season in Dallas was 1963, and I managed the Atlanta Crackers in 1964. We were bad, really bad. We lost our first nine in a row. The day we'd lost our eighth straight, I ran through a yellow light and got pulled over by an Atlanta cop. Figures.

He asked who I was and what I did for a living, and I told him I managed the Crackers.

"I'll let you go," he said. "You've got enough troubles with that team."

I used to spend my winters managing in Puerto Rico, where the baseball was a little backward. One day I took pitcher Dennis Lamp out of a game and sent him back to the trainer's room to ice his shoulder. Lamp came back five minutes later complaining that we didn't have any ice.

"Hell, Dennis, there's tons of ice in there," I said.

"Yeah," he said, "but the trainer says that ice is for the beer."

Oh.

Listen, my trainer in Puerto Rico that year was a real gem. At first I thought he was a normal guy, because when guys would get hit by a pitch or something, he'd run out and spray ethyl chloride on them.

Or so I thought. One day, a kid hurt his ankle, and when I went out to take a quick look, my trainer was spraying the injury with bug spray.

"Oh, Skip," he'd say. "It works great."

Whatever.

One winter, I took over the Arecibo, Puerto Rico, team in mid-season. They weren't very good. One day, I smelled food cooking, and I couldn't figure out where it was coming from. That is, until I saw smoke coming from the back of the dugout. I turned around and found a bunch of the players cooking crabs and fish while the game was going on.

"What the hell's going on?" I screamed. "No wonder you guys are in last place."

I got rid of the cooks in short order.

I was in Puerto Rico when Roberto Clemente died in a plane crash on his way to Nicaragua. It was a sad thing, and the people mourned their hero for days.

But it got to be a little extreme, I thought. A few days after Clemente's death, four of my Latin players were saying, "Yak (they called me 'Yak' instead of 'Jack'), we cannot play. Our hero's body has not been found. We don't want to play."

I explained to them that Clemente's body might never be found.

"Well, Yak," they said, "we are mourning him. We cannot play."

I told them I was gonna fine each of them $200. But I also said that if they felt so strongly about Clemente, I'd donate their money to the Clemente Memorial Fund.

And I also said, "You guys better be at the 9 o'clock memorial service they're having for Clemente tonight. If you feel that strongly, you should go pray with the people."

Well, we had a game that night, and I looked up and saw all four of them up in the stands drinking beer.

I doubled their fine and gave it all to the Clemente Fund.

For sure, Puerto Rican ball never lacked intrigue. The fans there, they'd bet on anything and everything. They'd bet on pitches, stolen bases, you name it. One night, I was bringing out the lineup card, and I heard, "Bang! Bang!" I looked up, and saw one guy chasing another guy, and one of the guys had blood spilling out from his chest. Seems they'd had a bet the night before, and the loser hadn't paid up.

Whatever.

Spoonie was afraid of everything that moved, including fly balls. Guys would stick lizards or garden snakes in Spoonie's uniform pants or in his shoes or even in his jockstrap. Spoonie would jump 15 feet when he'd see these snakes. Spoonie always jumped 15 feet when he got scared.

5
Spoonie
(Here's a Real
Funny Part)

CHUCK WEATHERSPOON. HMMMMM. What can I say about Spoonie that we can print here? Let's see. Spoonie, he was afraid of anything and everything that moved. That about says it.

Truthfully, Spoonie was probably the most fun-loving player I ever managed. We acquired him from the Giants back when I was in Missoula, and he played for me from 1956 to 1963 in a whole mess of different cities. I kept bringing him with me because I needed the comic relief.

Spoonie was a black man, about 6′4″, 200 pounds. If we'd had the designated hitter back then, he would've made it to the big leagues. I think he hit 32 homers for me one year in Missoula.

But, as I've said, Spoonie was afraid of everything that moved, including fly balls. I stuck him in right field for a game in Green Bay, and there was a slight upgrade near the right-field fence. A ball got hit his way, and Spoonie went back, back, back. Finally, he reached the upgrade and fell flat on his rear. His head banged against the outfield wall, and he was seeing stars.

Somehow, the ball came right at him and landed in his glove.

Lee Stange, our pitcher, came running out and said, "You made it look so easy, Spoonie."

Another day in Vancouver, a fly ball hit a bird flying overhead in right field. Spoonie, who didn't always know which end was up, caught the bird instead of the ball.

In Missoula, guys liked getting to the ballpark early so they could fiddle around with Spoonie's stuff. Guys would go fishing and stick the dead fish in Spoonie's car trunk. They'd stick lizards or garden snakes in Spoonie's uniform pants or in his shoes or even in his jockstrap.

Spoonie would jump 15 feet when he'd see these snakes. Spoonie always jumped 15 feet when he got scared.

I remember a night when Spoonie was rooming with Aaron Jones, a 6'5" black pitcher from Chicago. Those were the unfortunate days when black guys roomed with black guys and white guys roomed with white guys. Though some of our white players begged to room with Spoonie because he was a great guy and because they loved scaring him and watching him take that 15-foot leap.

Anyway, Spoonie and Jones were together on this particular night. I came by to do a bedcheck, and they were just sitting around eating candy. Suddenly, we heard a sound like an owl.

"Oooooooooooo! Oooooooooooo!"

Jonesy's eyes lit up and so did Spoonie's.

"You hear something?" Jonesy said.

"Yeah," Spoonie said.

"You go look," Jonesy said.

"No, you go look," Spoonie said.

I looked. I went over to the window and saw two of my players with white bed sheets over their heads, making them look like ghosts.

I turned back toward Spoonie and Jonesy and said, "Don't see nothin'."

And I left.

I closed the door behind me, but peeked back through the keyhole.

"Ooooooooooo! Oooooooooooo!"

It was the "ghosts" again.

Finally, Spoonie went over to the window and saw the two supposed ghosts.

He jumped his 15 feet.

So did Jonesy.

Then they ran out the door.

I ran to the window and directed the ghosts inside. "One of you get under the bed and one of you get in the bathtub," I said.

Spoonie and Jonesy finally reappeared, warily, and I told them, "Looks like the coast's clear."

So they plopped down on their beds. Jonesy, who had kept the box of candy on the floor between the two beds, reached down for a piece.

The candy was gone. A ghost had pulled it under the bed.

"Spoonie, what'd you do with the candy?" asked Jonesy.

"Nothin'," Spoonie said.

They were getting kind of paranoid, so I left. But I peeked through the keyhole again and saw Spoonie walk into the bathroom. He turned on the light, and

I heard the howl: "Oooooooooooo! Oooooooooooo!"

Spoonie jumped his 15 feet.

A few years later, I accepted a job with the Atlanta Crackers, and I took Spoonie with me. At that point, he was 35 or 36 or 37 or 45. No one knew because he wouldn't say. Every year, though, the press guide said he was 30. He was 30 for three straight seasons, and he was 29 the fourth year.

Well, one day we were playing an exhibition against an Atlanta prison team, and we had to walk through the prison to get to the field. The inmates— who were all behind bars—kept hollering and making fun of our uniforms. I didn't really mind it, and then I got this terrible, wonderful idea.

I went over to one of them and I said, "Hey, we've got this guy Chuck Weatherspoon. He's from Pine- land, Texas, and we're always kidding him about his age. When he gets here, holler at him like you know him. I'll say, 'Do you know this guy?,' and you'll go on to say you went to school with him.

"I'll ask you how old he is, and you'll say 36."

Well, that's exactly what he did. Spoonie kept say- ing, "Skip, Skip. I don't know this guy."

Eventually, we made it out to the field for the game. I was at the plate being a ham, and, when I batted, I pointed out to dead center field like Babe Ruth did. It got to be ball 3, and I told the ump not to let me walk. Finally, the prison-team pitcher threw one over the plate, and I actually put it over the fence. The first-base coach fainted.

Anyway, we won the game, and I asked Spoonie to pick up the equipment. Since he was a catcher, that was his job. But I got another terrible, wonderful idea. I hurried the rest of the guys up, making sure Spoonie would be the last to leave. Then I asked a prison guard to help me with a gag: I asked him to throw Spoonie in an empty prison cell.

Sure enough, Spoonie came walking through the prison carrying all the equipment when the guard said, "Where the hell did you get that uniform?"

And he threw him in a cell.

Spoonie was screaming, "Skip, Skip!"

I said, "Hey, he's not with us."

I remember another day when a guy hung a live lobster over Spoonie's locker. I backed him over to his cubicle and said, "Sit down, Spoonie."

This lobster was about to nip his ear off, but he didn't notice.

I said, "Spoonie, got any chew?"

"Yeah, Skip," he said. And when he turned to get some, he saw the lobster's claws.

He jumped his 15 feet.

But most of all, Spoonie hated snakes. I remember going up to Northern Montana to play an exhibition against the Cuban Giants. Our trip took us through some back roads, and one street sign said, "Do not leave car. Rattlesnakes roaming." We actually could see the snakes on the road. Spoonie saw one, screamed, and jumped his 15 feet to the back of the bus.

So that gave our players some ideas. In Salt Lake City, one guy gave the opposing first baseman a rubber snake to leave lying near the bag. Spoonie, who was playing first that day, ran out onto the field, saw the snake, and jumped his 15 feet into the first-base coaching box.

One year when I was managing Wilson, North Carolina, we saw in the papers that a real snake had been spotted in right field during a game in Raleigh. Our next trip happened to be to Raleigh. Spoonie didn't want to go. But I made him go, and I even played him in right. In the second inning, I got ahold of Raleigh's first-base coach and asked him to tell his rightfielder to warn Spoonie that he'd seen a snake out there.

Well, Spoonie got the warning, and suddenly I had two second basemen. Spoonie wouldn't go to right field.

I called time.

"Spoonie, get out there," I said.

"No," he said.

"Don't worry," I said. "You'll be okay."

So he slowly made his way out there, looking between his legs and over his shoulders for the snake while our pitcher was throwing. If anybody hit one out there, it was a sure triple.

The next inning, I told my centerfielder to inch over toward right-center and discreetly toss some pebbles behind Spoonie. Spoonie heard the pebbles fly by and thought it was the snake.

Fifteen feet.

Another time, the guys snuck into Spoonie's hotel room and put a rubber snake under his pillow. But a maid found the snake before Spoonie did, and she collapsed and had a heart attack.

I had to tell the guys to cool it.

Spoonie used to bum cigars off of me, and most of our players knew that. One day, a couple of guys were fooling around with my cigar collection, and I didn't know why. Anyway, that afternoon Spoonie came to my office to grab a cigar. He lit up while he drove home, and the cigar exploded.

Spoonie plowed into the car in front of him.

There was another day when our bus broke down on the way to Missoula. It was 4 A.M., and nobody was around on the highway. A bunch of the guys got restless and climbed out of the bus. They found a huge pasture nearby full of horses, and they started riding around bareback. One of the guys found a stick with a nail in it, and he stuck Spoonie's horse in the rear end.

The horse threw Spoonie 15 feet.

In Missoula one day, we played a donkey baseball game. You know, you hit the ball and ride a donkey around the bases. We gave Spoonie a donkey that wouldn't move. He hit the ball, and his donkey just stood there. Spoonie kicked it and kicked it and kicked it. Wouldn't move.

In Spoonie's second at-bat, we gave him the wildest donkey. Spoonie hit the ball, and his donkey took off.

Spoonie got tossed 15 feet.

Later, in 1969, I actually managed *against* Spoonie. I was in Omaha, and he was in Denver—we'd never been on opposite teams before. They sent him up as a pinch hitter, and he dug in real good. I mean, he'd dug a 4-inch hole with his spikes. I saw a rake in the dugout, so I tossed it out on the field.

"Hell, Weatherspoon!" I screamed. "As long as you're gardening, why don't you use this?"

He struck out on three pitches.

"You screwed me up, Skip," he said afterward.

Eventually, Spoonie and I drifted apart. But I got a letter from him when I was managing the Royals. He'd been injured on the job and hadn't received his workman's compensation check. He needed 500 bucks.

I sent him the money because, after all, he gave me more than 500 bucks in effort and entertainment.

I really, really loved the guy. I remember the time

in Fox Cities when he saved my little sister's life. I had invited my mom and dad to visit me there, and they'd brought little Kathy, who was about 10 years old. We stopped by at the home of our team physician, a Dr. Fred Marshall, who had a pool in his backyard. Spoonie was there, too. I told Kathy she could take a swim, but how'd I know she couldn't swim? She'd had a bathing suit with her, so I sent her to the pool.

She got in water over her head and panicked. Spoonie saw it all happening through a window and jumped in to save her.

For once, I was glad to see him jump 15 feet.

I needed to go to my bullpen. I chose some-one else, not Koudis. But I hurt his feelings. So he got dressed and drove away. Went to a movie.

6
Don Koudis
(This Part Is Just
as Funny)

IF IT'S NOT one thing, it's another. In 1960 when I was at Wilson, we signed a big, lanky, lefty pitcher named Don Koudis. He'd been with the Burlington Indians, who played in our league, and he used to give us fits.

Problem was, he kept giving us fits after we signed him. When we got him, we told him to report immediately to our general manager, Dickie Harris. He called Harris on the phone, but Harris was out playing golf. So Koudis went to find him. He took a cab to the golf course. He didn't know if Harris was on the first hole or the 15th, so he just started walking.

It was 100 degrees, one of the hottest days of the year. But for some reason, Koudis was wearing a gray business suit. He walked all the way to the seventh hole and still hadn't found Harris, who just happened to be on the eighth green at the time. But when Koudis got to the eighth, Harris was on the

73

ninth. When Koudis got to the ninth, Harris was on the tenth. And so on.

Koudis finally gave up. I was sitting in the baseball office with the club president, and Koudis walked in, his business suit soaking wet.

"Couldn't find Harris," he said.

Koudis didn't have a bad arm, as long as you took him out after four or five innings. By the sixth inning, his fastball would be a change-up.

So I stuck him in the bullpen. He had great success as a short reliever as long as he didn't have to field a ball or make a catch or anything important like that. I remember him pitching in a tight game when the other team had runners on first and third. I knew a double steal was in the works, so I called time and approached the mound. Spoonie was my catcher, so there stood the three of us: Koudis, Spoonie, and I.

I told Koudis plain and simple, "Listen, if the guy on first breaks for second, Spoonie's gonna throw you the ball. And you turn around real quick to see if the guy on third breaks for home. If he does, throw to Spoonie and nail him. Got it?"

"Sure, Skip!" Koudis said.

So the guy broke for second and Spoonie threw to Koudis, who immediately ducked.

It hit him in the head.

The run scored.

"What happened, Don?" I asked.

"I forgot what to do," he said.

Then he pouted. His feelings were hurt. His feelings were always hurt.

One game, Burlington had us down, 10–2, in the fourth inning, and I needed to go to my bullpen. I chose someone else, not Koudis. I wasn't gonna use my ace reliever when we were so far behind. But I hurt his feelings. So, little did I know, Koudis took off. He got dressed and drove away. Went to a movie.

In the meantime, the game got close. It was 10–8. I signaled for Koudis to warm up, but he was nowhere to be found. I had to use my best pitcher, Lee Stange, our 20-game winner, and we ended up winning, 14–12.

I got a call at 2 A.M. that night. It was Koudis.

"Skip, you mad at me?"

"No," I said. "I'm just disappointed."

"I didn't think you had confidence in me, Skip."

"You're my ace, damnit!" I said.

"But you didn't use me in a 10–2 game," he said. "You needed me."

"Just show up tomorrow," I said.

He never showed.

Our team bus was going back to Wilson that day, a two-and-a-half-hour drive. Koudis and I were staying at the same hotel in Wilson, and he was there when I arrived.

"How'd you get here?" I demanded.

"I saw today's game, Skip," he said. "I was there. But I didn't want to ride the bus. I knew you were mad. So, I called the Highway Patrol and asked them to take me to the Durham County Line. And then I asked the Highway Patrol to take me to the Wilson County Line. They did it for free."

What could I say?

Koudis had it in for the women. He'd talk to every gal on the street. And he was always sneaking away with some lady. I always told him I had spies watching him, and he believed me. That's because Koudis used to tell his roommates all about his dates, and his roommates would tell me. So I'd be telling Koudis where he'd been the night before.

One of my pitchers was Jim Rantz, who is now the

Twins' farm director. One day in Winston-Salem, Rantz and I decided to really follow him. Koudis was a nervous guy to begin with—he'd always be jumping and turning around, always looking around as if someone was following him.

Well, we were trailing him that night, about 30 or 40 feet behind. Whenever he'd turn around and look, we'd duck into a store front. We once ducked into a pawn shop doorway, and suddenly police lights were on us. We didn't know it, but there'd been a rash of robberies at pawn shops, and the cops were checking us out. Hell, we didn't know what was going on. We explained who we were following and so forth, but by that time Koudis had gotten away.

Another night, a bunch of our players were in a bar, and Koudis was putting the moves on some barmaid. She agreed to meet him at another bar at midnight, so he left.

About five of my guys followed him outside. He twitched and turned around, and he saw them. He started running, so they ran, too. He jumped into a phone booth, but that just made it easier for them to catch him.

A cab drove by, so he hopped out of the phone booth and hailed it. One of the guys, Snyder, ran for the cab, too. Koudis grabbed one door and Snyder grabbed the other.

"This is my cab," Koudis said.

"It's mine," Snyder said.

"It's neither of yours," the cabbie said, and he drove off.

Koudis took off again. Meanwhile, the rest of the guys hailed another cab and said, "Follow that guy!"

Koudis was darting from one side of the street to the other, and the cabbie began saying to his dispatcher, "I picked these guys up, and I don't know where the hell I'm going. I've been shot at in the war. I've been wounded. But this is worse!"

Koudis finally lost them.

At that point, Koudis still thought I might have detectives following him. Of course I didn't, but I had ordered a bunch of my guys to keep an eye on him. I told them to write down everything he did.

One day, they were all out playing miniature golf, and Koudis stopped to talk to two gals in a blue Chevy. He got their phone numbers on a pink piece of paper and stuck it in his shirt pocket. My guys wrote everything down. At 10:10 A.M., he'd do this; at 10:15, he'd do that; at 10:30, he'd talk to two girls. And so on.

That night at the ballpark, I asked Koudis what he'd done that day.

"Oh, I don't know, Skip," he said.

"You played golf, right?" I said.

He nodded.

"Did you talk to any gals?" I asked.

"No, no, no," he said. "No way, Skip."

"Yes, you did," I said. "You talked to two gals in a blue Chevy."

"Oh yeah, that's right," he said, looking nervous.

"Did you get their phone numbers?" I asked.

"No, no, no. No way, Skip." He was starting to sweat.

"Let's go in and check your shirt pocket," I said.

I pulled out the pink piece of paper.

"God damn, Skip," he screamed, "you *do* have detectives!"

So Koudis began sneaking out in the middle of the night, roaming the streets. Back in those days, we had a tight budget, so everybody had to have a roommate. One night, Koudis roomed with "Peg Leg" Bates, our bus driver at Wilson who had a wooden leg. Well, Peg Leg used to take his leg off at night and stick it beside his bed. And one morning after he'd roomed with Koudis, I got a frantic phone call from Peg Leg.

"I can't find my leg! Koudis took it! Koudis took it! I can't get outta bed!"

I rushed to his room and found the wooden leg on the top shelf of the closet. Koudis had gone out roaming the streets and stuck it up there.

All the players used to get all over Peg Leg. One bus ride, he got angry and called them a worthless bunch of ballplayers. He said they were making too much noise for him to drive. It kinda upset me, and I said, "Peg Leg, you drive the bus, and I'll run this club. My players don't have to put up with that crap."

He pulled over and jumped out.

"If you don't like it," he screamed, "find someone else to drive the bus!"

"Fine," I said. "Can anyone drive this bus?"

Spoonie volunteered.

So we left poor Peg Leg 45 miles down the road. We thought that was the last of him, but he hitched a ride and showed up a few minutes before that night's game began. He apologized. And we never heard a word out of him again.

Anyway, back to Koudis. He was always talking on the telephone. Whenever our bus stopped for gas, he'd be the first one out to make a call. So I bought an old pay phone and put it inside the bus. It didn't work or anything, but we put a sign over it: "Koudis's Private Phone."

Yeah, we had a lot of fun at his expense. He was

just so paranoid. For instance, Rantz started pitching great, and I made him my short reliever instead of Koudis. Again, I'd hurt Koudis's feelings.

Koudis went around telling his teammates that "Rantz is the skipper's bobo, his pet." He'd also say, "Hell, I bet Rantz is in there shining the skipper's shoes."

I got another terrible, wonderful idea. I actually had Rantz shine my shoes for a joke. I told the rest of the guys to get Koudis.

"Koudis! Koudis!" they said. "Rantz is shining the skip's shoes, just like you said."

Koudis came running in, and there we were. We didn't see him again the rest of the day.

Koudis loved to coach first base. In our half of the inning, he'd run out there as fast as he could. Well, at this point, he still thought Rantz was my bobo, so I continued to have fun with him.

I put Rantz in charge of the first-base coaches.

I told Rantz to say, "Hey, our first-base coaches aren't getting out there fast enough." That night, Koudis sprinted out there as fast as he could, but Rantz stood up and said, "Koudis, that's not good enough! Come back in here."

Koudis was fed up. He called a team meeting, inviting everyone but Rantz and me. Of course, the rest of the guys let us know about the meeting, and we snuck in and listened through the door. He was telling them, "The skip is playing favorites!"

I told Rantz I was gonna type Koudis's release. It wouldn't be official, but I was gonna fake him out. So I brought him into my office. "Here you go," I said, handing him his release. "You're gone."

He put his head down, walked out, and took off his uniform. He showered, got dressed, and was getting ready to leave. He'd believed me, but, hell, I really needed the guy.

I told Rantz to talk to him. Rantz went up to him and said, "Anything I can do?"

Koudis said, "I sure would like to play."

Rantz said, "Well, I'll talk to Jack."

A few minutes later, I brought Koudis back into my office, and he said he wanted to stay. I answered, "Let me go ask Rantz if he wants you back." Koudis freaked out.

Rantz came in and said, "Koudis, suit up."

We were really playing this thing up. On the bus, I'd always fill out a report on my players to send to the Twins' front office. I'd have Rantz sit with me when I did it, and Koudis would always sit behind us, trying to see the reports. I knew what he was doing, so I filled out some fake ones. On Rantz, I put down things like, "Can't-miss prospect. Could be best ever. Bring him up as soon as possible."

And for Koudis, I'd write, "Poor fastball, poor breaking ball, poor everything."

Poor Koudis. He'd pout.

That whole season, he said he was gonna straighten out. He said he'd met a nice girl named Mary, and they were getting married after the season. Well, the season ended, and I got this call from this Mary. She said "You don't know me, but I'm trying to get ahold of one of your players—Don Koudis."

I had no idea where he was. I thought he was in Chicago, but I told her to check with the team president. She said she'd already tried that. And she went on to say that they were gonna get married and that she'd been sending him money every month to buy a wedding ring. She said he'd finally bought the ring and given it to her over a romantic dinner. But it didn't fit, so he took it back to be sized.

The next day, she said, Koudis gave the ring to her best friend.

She wanted to find him so she could kill him.

Deep down, though, Koudis wasn't a bad guy. I remember a game in Greensboro when we'd had a beanball war. Tempers flared, and I was worried there might be a serious brawl. After the game, I told our players to go straight to the bus and by no means to go near the opposing clubhouse. Well, I got dressed, walked out the clubhouse door, and there was a huge fight going on outside. I rushed to break it up, but one of their guys grabbed me and was about to smack me.

Koudis stepped in front.

"Hey, I wouldn't dare hit my skipper if I were you," Koudis said.

Many years later, when I was managing the Royals, I noticed someone screaming at me from the stands. It was this big fat guy, about 300 pounds.

"Hey, Skip! Remember me!"

It was Koudis.

I was never boring with the umps. I wore a Beatles wig when I exchanged my lineup card at home plate. The ump wanted to throw me out, but I said, "You can't tell me how to wear my hair."

7
You're Out!
(Of Your Mind)

I'VE BEEN KNOWN to bend an umpire's ear or two or three. But that's because some umpires bend the rules.

Let me introduce Joe Ring, an umpire who had a permanent black cloud over his head. Every time I saw Joe Ring—and it was more often than I cared to—something ludicrous happened. I remember a game against Great Falls in Missoula when I was player-manager. One of their outfielders—a guy named Greenwald—smacked a home run, but I was catching and noticed that he'd barely touched the corner of home plate. Not that I was a troublemaker, but I screamed, "Hey, he missed home!"

The ump was Joe Ring.

And Joe said, "No, he didn't miss home, pardner." Joe always said pardner. Hell, he wasn't my pardner.

I said, "Joe! Which game are you watching?"

Joe stood there a minute, rubbed his brow, and he

said, "You're right, pardner. He missed home."

Right away, I asked Joe for a ball. I'd put it in play at the pitcher's rubber, and I'd step on home plate. But Joe said, "Nah, pardner. I'll just give you a ball, and you can appeal."

That wasn't the rule, but, hell, Joe seemed to know what he was doing. He gave me a ball, I stepped on home plate, and Joe ran over to the Great Falls dugout, screaming, *"Yooooooooou're ouuuuuuuttta theeeeeere!"*

Their dugout went wild. Stan Waziak, the Great Falls manager, filed a protest because we hadn't put the ball in play at the rubber. I knew Stan was right, too. But, hell, I was gonna try to pull this thing off.

Joe listened to Stan's argument, and then he came to me and said, "Pardner, this is what we're gonna do." Now get this: he had talked Stan into putting Greenwald somewhere on the third-base line, about 40 feet from home plate. He'd put the ball in play at the mound, and Greenwald would try to score. I know it sounds unbelievable, but I've got witnesses.

Anyway, Joe gave us a couple minutes to warm up. My pitcher threw me a couple fastballs, but I never threw back the last warm-up pitch. I kept it in my catcher's mitt.

Finally, Ring said, "Is everybody ready? Play ball!"

Greenwald took off, but I already had the ball in my glove, so I just tagged him. Ring screamed, "You're out again!"

Well, Stan went nuts again and filed a protest. We had to start all over again the next night.

And that next night, Joe was the first-base umpire. In the fifth inning, we were behind by three runs, and I was on second base. Sandy Valdespino hit a grounder to the first baseman, who tossed it to the pitcher covering first. It was a close play, but Joe called Sandy safe.

Their whole team charged poor Joe. Meanwhile, I was circling third and coming home. Suddenly, the home-plate ump, Carl Panosh, called time.

I argued, seeing as how I was about to score.

Joe and Carl conferred for a few minutes, and then Joe came over and said, "Pardner, back to third."

I said, "Pardner, I'm protesting."

Joe said, "Hold it." And he had another meeting with Carl. Then he turned around and said, "Pardner, you score!"

True story. Got witnesses.

OK, OK, I kind of instigated some of these things. But Joe used to get so confused. Here's an example: my pitchers at Missoula used to get killed on 0-and-2 counts. Instead of wasting a pitch, they'd try sneaking in a strike, and the batter would be all over it. So I started fining my pitchers 10 bucks if they threw an 0-and-2 strike.

One night, Dick Schultz was my pitcher, and he went 0 and 2 on a hitter. On purpose, he threw a ball way high.

Joe Ring called strike three.

Dick Schultz was steaming. He charged Joe, screaming, "That was no strike. That was high." He'd just struck someone out, and yet he was nearly crying.

"Pardner, you're nuts," Joe said.

Later, I had to explain to Joe that Schultzie was just trying to save himself 10 bucks.

Another night, I'd already lost my starting second baseman to an injury, and then my backup second baseman, Addie Hintze, got hit in the wrist with a fastball. He started hopping around in pain, but the ump—who else but Joe Ring—said the ball had hit Hintze's bat, not his wrist.

"Pardner, that's a foul ball," he said.

I argued like hell, but to no avail. Hintze was my last player, so I had to leave him in the game with the bum wrist. He actually batted one-handed.

Afterward, we took Addie to the hospital, and they said he'd fractured it. To soothe Hintze's feelings, we all went out for a bite to eat.

In walked Joe Ring.

Joe, who just never had a clue, saw Hintze and said, "What happened, Hintze?"

"Ah, I fell down the stairs," Hintze said sarcastically.

But Joe never caught on. He said, "Pardner, you better take care of yourself better."

Another time, I noticed that the opposing manager forgot to include one of his catchers on the roster, which is illegal. Sure, it's picky, but, hey, you do what you've gotta do. So I didn't say a word; I just waited for the ineligible player to play and then I'd protest.

Anyway, Joe threw me out of the game for arguing a strike call, and I appointed Spoonie acting manager. Their ineligible player still hadn't played, but I told Spoonie we were gonna get them. Finally, this ineligible player pinch hit. I wasn't gonna say anything unless he got a hit. He struck out, but then he stayed in the game. So I told Spoonie to protest.

Well, sure enough, he wasn't on the roster, and the opposing manager was running after Spoonie and cursing at me, too.

After the game, I saw Joe Ring in a restaurant and I said, "Go ahead and fine me for getting kicked out, Joe. But you didn't do your job, Joe. You didn't even know that player was ineligible. You should've checked your roster. I'm gonna file a report on you, Joe."

Joe said, "Pardner, if you don't send in your report, I won't send in mine." I agreed.

Every once in a while, if my team was getting blown out, I'd go out and pitch. I was no Dizzy Dean, believe me. One day I gave up a long home run down the right-field line. It was fair by about three feet, but I screamed, "Foul ball! Foul ball!"

Joe Ring stood there a moment, scratched his brow, and said, "Pardner, that's a foul ball!" The batter was slightly disturbed, and he ended up grounding into a double play.

Well, two weeks later, we played the same team, and I hit a home run at least 20 feet fair. The opposing catcher—still angry about the last time—screamed, "Foul ball! Foul ball!"

Joe Ring called it foul.

I was fuming, but what could I do? Later that game, I got ahold of another pitch and put it over the fence in right-center field. I stood and watched it, and then turned toward Joe: "Hey, Joe. Is that fair or not? I'm not gonna run the bases just for my health."

He called it fair.

I think the maddest I ever got was in 1960, but it wasn't because of Joe Ring. It was another ump, Tommy Simon.

I was managing, and the bases were loaded for my first baseman Ray Looney. Ray cracked one down the first-base line, over the first baseman's head and fair by a good two yards. Then it swerved into the right-field corner. Naturally, I was waving all three runners in, but when I looked up, I saw Looney running straight toward Simon.

Simon had called it foul.

Looney nearly killed him. But I pushed Looney

out of the way and said, "No, let me kill him."

Simon explained that he hadn't seen the ball right away. And when he'd finally seen it, the ball was in foul territory, so he called it foul.

Well, he'd already kicked Looney out of the game (Looney kept jawing at him), and I just tried to reason with him. I said, "Check with your partner. Check with your partner."

Simon wouldn't do it. Instead, he said if Looney apologized, he could stay in the game. I needed Looney, who was one of my best hitters, so I told him to apologize.

Looney walked up to Simon and said, "I apologize . . . But I don't mean it."

That was still good enough for Simon. Looney stayed in the game, but he hit into a double play. The game eventually went into extra innings and was called on account of curfew.

I was really hot and bothered. Everyone on our team was. The umpires had screwed us out of a game, and now we had to play a doubleheader the next day. I hardly had any rested pitchers.

A few minutes afterward, Simon walked into our clubhouse.

"What the hell you doing here?" I said. "Get the hell outta here!"

He said, "No, I want to come in and apologize. I screwed you guys up." Hell, we were already mad enough. I told Rantz to get the door, and I got Simon by the seat of his pants and tossed him out.

He got up, dusted himself off, and said, "You ain't so tough."

I said, "You stick your head in here one more time, and you'll really see how tough I am."

And he left. Never heard another word out of him.

Basically, I was never boring with the umps. When I managed the Atlanta Crackers in 1964, we got off to a horrible start—0 and 9. We finally won our first game in Buffalo, but then we went to Toronto and lost two out of three. To top it off, eight of my players got sick with the German measles in Toronto. The team was going on to Columbus, but we had to leave the sick guys behind in Toronto. We got to Columbus and lost the first game, 1-0, in 13 innings. The next day, some newspaper wrote that we and Columbus were the two most boring teams in baseball. I was steamed. I saw a novelty shop close to the hotel and decided to get even. I bought a Beatles wig (they were popular at the time), and I also bought a plastic golf club in case the umps were calling low-ball strikes that night. Last, I bought one of those light bulbs that would light when you touched it to any piece of metal. I spray painted the light bulb green. That way, if I wanted to, I could really give my hitters "the green light."

That night, I had a charming time. First, I wore my Beatles wig when I exchanged my lineup card at home plate. The ump wanted to throw me out, but I said, "You can't tell me how to wear my hair." Later, the umpires were calling low-ball strikes, so I hurled my plastic club onto the field. And I kept flashing my hitters the green light.

I got kicked out.

But we weren't boring.

"I'll give you 50 bucks to eat it," one of the guys told him. So Faul told the guys to wash off the frog and get him a cup of water. Then he picked it up, ate it, and spit out the bones.

8
Bill Faul
(This Part Is Gross)

BY 1969, I had hooked on with the expansion Kansas
City Royals. They made me their Triple-A manager
in Omaha, just one more step toward becoming a
big-league manager.

The thing about expansion teams is that you get a
lot of kids on their way up and a lot of older guys on
their way down.

Bill Faul, he was on his way down.

He had pitched with Detroit, and the Royals
plucked him away in the expansion draft. He didn't
make the major league club, so they sent him down
to me. Gee, thanks.

What can I say about Bill? Well, he had a good-
looking wife, a girl named Deems. And I noticed
that every once in a while, Deems would go walking
down near the bullpen. I kept wondering why.

I found out. Apparently, Faul had been teed off
that I hadn't used him and he had sent his wife for
his gun.

Yes, he was a little different. When he played in Detroit, he'd been afraid of flying, and he tried getting a hypnotist to cure him. I guess it didn't work, because when I got him, he used to request a wheelchair upon landing. Some of my guys would wheel him off, and then they'd push him with all their might. He'd go barreling through the terminal, a runaway wheelchair. *"Wooooooooweeeee!"* he'd scream. One time he crashed into a wall, and we all thought he was dead.

He'd sit in the bullpen, telling the rest of the guys how he'd shot people with his gun or how he'd bitten the head off a dog and a cat when he was a kid. Said he also used to eat live frogs.

The guys in the bullpen really believed him, and I told them to wise up. No way it was true. But they had to find out. So one night in Des Moines when the clubhouse runway was virtually flooded from a rainstorm the previous night, one of the guys found a frog, and brought it out to the bullpen.

It was time for Bill Faul to put up or shut up.

"I'll give you 50 bucks to eat it," one of the guys told him. So Faul told the guys to wash off the frog and get him a cup of water. Then he picked it up, ate it, and spit out the bones.

Jimmy Campanis—Al Campanis's son—came running in, screaming, "He ate it! He ate it! You won't believe it, Skip."

I didn't believe it. But, to make sure, I asked one of my relievers, Paul Epperson, who was very religious and honest. He never told a lie.

"Did he eat it, Paul?" I asked.

"Sure did, Skip."

Well, our next trip took us to Indianapolis, and now the guys had big plans. On the bus, they were offering Faul two nights with their girlfriends if he ate a bird. Another offered him 100 bucks to eat a white rat.

He took them up on both.

The minute we got to our Indianapolis hotel, five of the guys disappeared. They went to a pet store.

See, they were gonna let Faul pick out the parakeet he was gonna eat. And the white rat. He chose a blue parakeet, and the lady behind the counter asked, "Would you care for some bird food?"

Faul snapped, "It ain't gonna live that long."

We were playing a doubleheader that night. Faul was gonna eat the bird between games. When the first game ended, you've never seen such a rush for the clubhouse.

He stood there in the middle of the room, naked from the waist up. The parakeet was in the palm of his hand. Jimmy Campanis was doing the play by play:

Yes, ladies and gentlemen, he's looking at the parakeet, he's studying it . . .

All of a sudden, the parakeet pecked Faul on the wrist. "You SOB!" he screamed. In one motion, he grabbed it with two hands and bit its head off.

Feathers flew everywhere. I was a little nauseated.

The next night, he was supposed to eat the white rat. But the guys forgot that was the night of the major league All-Star game, and we had no game. So they stuck the white rat in a cardboard box. Faul would eat it the day after.

Well, we got back to the ballpark the day after the All-Star game, and the rat was gone. It had eaten its way out of the box. No one could find it. Faul was off the hook, as was the rat, at least for the moment.

But during the game, one of the guys found the rat

in the corner of the clubhouse. Since we were leaving for home after the game, there'd be no time for Faul to eat it. So as a joke, the guy just stuck the rat in Faul's pants pocket.

Now, Faul was one of these guys who never took a shower. Oh, he'd go into the shower room, but before the water hit the ground, he'd be out of there toweling off. He'd simply pull on his pants and leave before anyone else.

He did the same thing on this particular night, but when he pulled on his pants, he felt something wiggle. See, the rat had partly eaten its way through the lining of his pants. Faul felt this, dropped his pants, and started stomping on them. A few minutes later, he pulled out the dead rat and threw it in the trash.

He pulled up his pants and left.

Lou Piniella, today the Yankee general manager, was the most selfish player I've ever seen.

9
I Was Royalty
(For a While)

LET ME GO back and explain a few things. In 1964, I
managed the Atlanta Crackers—the Twins' Triple-A
team—but they were going nowhere, and Calvin
Griffith, the Twins' owner, made me his special-as-
signment scout.

Basically, I set up shop in the New Jersey area,
because my dad had just had a heart attack, and I
wanted to be around him. He needed help with his
business, someone to drive his taxis and his wreckers.

In my spare time, I scouted. I told them to draft a
kid named Steve Braun, who eventually hung around
the big league a while. And in 1965, I went down to
the Tampa–St. Petersburg area to see a kid named
Steve Garvey. I recommended him to the Twins, and
they drafted him that year. Garvey decided to go to
college and was later drafted by the Dodgers. You
know the rest.

At this point, my wife and kids were in North

Carolina. With me being away, they really had to sacrifice, but my father meant so much to me. All my street smarts I got from him, all my get-up-and-go. He's the reason I went anywhere in life.

In December of 1966, he died. I ran his business for a while, and then I sold it. Actually, it was my first deal.

See, when my father bought his garage, he bought from the American Oil Company, and there was an understanding that Amoco would be the only gas he could sell for the next 20 years. Well, there were 10 more years to go, which made it hard to sell the place. Still, I told this one group that I'd try to get the agreement with Amoco rescinded. If I did, my dad's place would cost $30,000. If not, it'd cost just $20,000. Hell, they figured Amoco would never give in. But I flew to Baltimore and met with the Amoco people and got them to take the restriction out. Sold it for $30,000.

My first of many deals.

Anyway, it was 1967, and I wanted to manage again. Kansas City had just been awarded a big-league franchise, and farm director Lou Gorman— now Boston's general manager—called and asked me if I'd scout for the Royals with the intention of becoming their first Triple-A manager in 1969. I agreed.

Omaha—our Triple-A city—was great for me. We won the pennant in both 1969 and 1970, and we had a lot of characters—not to mention Bill Faul.

For instance, there was this one day during the Junior World Series in 1970 against Syracuse, when we had an early morning layover in Chicago. All the guys went into an airport restaurant for breakfast. The service was abominable, as slow as could be.

So a couple of my players—Fran Healy and Dennis Paepke—waltzed into the kitchen and emptied huge piles of scrambled eggs and bacon and sausage and biscuits onto their plates. Then they walked out and served the whole team.

Healy was still hungry, though, so he went back for more. The people in the kitchen never said a word.

In that particular series, we had a lot of rain. One day, it rained all the way up until game time, so our bus was late leaving the hotel. My guys were so restless, they just stood under the canopy outside the hotel and watched the traffic go by. Then, some lady backed out of a parking space and ran into a city bus. It was just a fender bender, but the bus driver got out to talk to the lady anyway.

In the meantime, Dennis Paepke—who was completely bored—walked onto the bus and told everyone to get off. "We've got a new bus coming for you," he said. "C'mon, c'mon. Everybody off."

Everybody piled off and stood in the rain.

Paepke, meanwhile, walked back under the canopy and watched them all get soaked.

That same year we clinched our playoff spot with two games left in the regular season, a Saturday and a Sunday. Saturday's game was rained out, but all the players stuck around for a few drinks. They went up to the Hit 'n' Run Room, a lounge for season-ticket holders.

Well, I left at about 5 o'clock, and they were feeling pretty good. Doc Ewing, our team physician, was there, and I told Doc to make sure the place got locked up.

Later that night, though, the guys were still there, and they decided they didn't want to play Sunday's game against Iowa. First they brought the security guard up to the Hit 'n' Run Room, and they got him so smashed he passed out. Then they hosed the entire field with water. For hours.

The next morning, it was beautiful outside. Every place in the city was dry except for the stadium field, which was flooded. My pitching coach, Galen Cisco, and I got pretty suspicious when we saw a bunch of divots in the infield dirt.

Hell, we decided we were gonna play this game. We brought out some gasoline, and we burned the field. Finally we got it to the point that we could play on it, except for an area behind second base that was still on fire. One of the Iowa players, José Tartabull, got the hose to put out the fire, which flooded the field again.

The game got called.

And the poor security guard had a helluva hangover.

In those days, I'd do anything to promote a ballgame. I was friendly with the Tulsa owner, A. Ray Smith, and he once asked me to drum up some excitement at his ballpark. Hell, I told him I used to get a little ticked off at his organ player, who'd always start pounding away when my pitcher was winding up. I mean, it didn't bother me that much, but I told him I could have some fun with it.

So that night we were leading, 6-0, and I nodded to A. Ray, who went up and told his organ player to start playing.

"God damn," I said to my players, who didn't know I was just joking, "that organ player always gives me fits."

Then, I ran out on the field and started complaining to the ump. "God darnit! That organ player is the reason we always have trouble here! Tell him to stop!"

The music stopped.

Then I nodded to A. Ray again, and the music started up.

Now I was going haywire, putting on one hell of a show. Warren Spahn—the Tulsa manager—was trying to stop the music because the umpire was about to forfeit the game to us if the music didn't stop. The next day in the papers, headlines screamed: "McKeon Doesn't Appreciate Music." On the TV interviews, I said, "Hey, I took a lot of courses in college, but not Music Appreciation."

The next night, 3,000 people packed the ballpark carrying bugles and horns, and they blew them every time my pitcher went into his windup. A. Ray Smith loved it. But I wasn't so sure I liked it.

A. Ray asked me to do him another favor later that year. He had brought in a television crew to shoot a commercial, and he wanted me to get into a big argument for the cameras. But there was one hitch, he said. The camera crew could only stay through the fifth inning.

"A. Ray," I said, "I can't just make up something. But hell, OK, I'll try."

Nothing eventful happened the first four innings. But I had no choice. I ran out and started jawing with the first-base umpire for no reason. Then, I ran down to the home-plate ump and started spraying tobacco juice all over him. The cameras got it all, but my players thought I was a lunatic.

I guess the greatest stunt of all was in 1969. Dave Blackwell, who was an Omaha sportscaster, wanted me to do something crazy for TV. And I came up with another terrible, wonderful idea. I decided we'd go to the zoo. There was an orangutan named Casey, and—with the approval of the zookeeper—we threw a baseball into his cage. He bit it, and started pounding his chest. I only thought gorillas pounded their chests, and only in the movies. But this was real. Dave had his cameraman shooting all of it. The orangutan was picking up the ball and throwing it against a wall. We threw a bat in his cage and—no kidding—he picked it up and put it on his shoulder like he was on deck or something. We got it all on camera. Finally, he took a bite out of the bat and sat down relatively close to the cameras. I had a contract and an Omaha cap in my hands, to make it look like I was gonna sign him up.

Anyway, that night Blackwell interviewed me on TV. He said, "Well, Jack, you're only four games in front, and the season's almost over. Do you need anything for pennant insurance?"

I answered, "Well, Dave, I've got a guy who's about 6′5″, 480 pounds. He's got a great arm and swings a mean bat. The only problem is his temper."

Blackwell said, "Well, Jack, can we take a look at him?"

And they rolled the film.

Those were some good times. Like the day in Oklahoma City when I was walking down the street with our broadcaster, Bill Beck, who is now the Padres' director of media relations. A beggar came up to us and asked for a quarter. I grabbed him by the lapel and shouted, "God damnit! I'm working this side of the street!"

He apologized and ran to the other side.

Anyway, we won a hell of a lot of games in Omaha. We had Paul Splittorff and Fran Healy and Al Fitzmorris and more. By 1971, my name was being linked to the Royals' big-league job. Bob Lemon, the Royal manager at the time, asked me if I wanted to go on a road trip with the team late in the 1971 season, but I turned him down. I thought there'd be too much conjecture if I did.

In 1972, Lemon asked again. I was in Kansas City at the time, giving them my minor-league evaluation report, and I was gonna turn Bob down again. But he insisted I go to California with them. I said, "Fine, if it's OK with Cedric Tallis."

Tallis, the team's general manager, was a little hesitant about it. I couldn't figure out why. But I went ahead anyway.

I joined the team in Minnesota. And when I arrived I picked up a paper and saw the headline: "McKeon To Replace Lemon As Royals' Manager."

Oh no.

I knew nothing about it, but I called Bob in his room to say I'd better go home. He said the article was nonsense and that I should stick around. So I did.

The trip to California was nice, and about four days after I flew home to North Carolina, Tallis phoned me.

"When can you get to K.C., Jack?

"I've just been there, Cedric."

"Come back. You're gonna be our manager."

So back I went. I met with the owner, Ewing Kauffman, and we got it all settled. But I hardly knew what I was getting myself into.

First of all, I was Kauffman's choice. His and only his. Cedric Tallis wanted Bob Lemon, and so did Lou Gorman, the farm director. The media didn't want me either, not the writers, not the broadcasters. They loved Lemon. No matter what I did, I wouldn't be better than Bob Lemon.

To this day, Bob Lemon and I remain friends. He

has never once intimated that I back-stabbed him or did anything to undermine him. One person, however, thinks I did.

His name is Lou Piniella.

Lou Piniella, today the Yankee general manager, was the most selfish player I've ever seen. When I took over that team in 1973, they were a bunch of .300 hitters that couldn't win. They worried about their batting averages, and that was it. They didn't move runners on second base with less than two outs. They couldn't bunt. They didn't steal bases. They hit .300.

In my first spring training, I lectured them every morning on baseball. A couple veterans thought it was a waste, but mainly it was Lou Piniella. I spoke about fundamentals, about smart baseball.

Lou wanted to go out and take batting practice.

Not everyone was that way. Amos Otis and John Mayberry listened attentively and did it my way. We ran more, sacrificed more, and won more. We finished in second place to the eventual World Champion Oakland A's.

But Lou hit only .250 that year. It was his worst season, and he blamed it on me. He said I stressed everything but hitting. Hell, we had batting practice every day. And there's no doubt that Lou Piniella could hit. I'm not saying he couldn't. But he's the one who undermined me. He once missed a team flight to Minnesota and I fined him $100 as I would any other player. In the past, the team had waited for Lou, but I was going to have rules. Lou went to Cedric Tallis and complained. He asked for his money back. Tallis gave it to him.

In his own book, Piniella claims I "greased the skids" for the firing of Bob Lemon. I did what? He says I came with the team at the end of the 1972 season and sat in the press box second-guessing Bob Lemon. I did what? He says I talked to sportswriters purposely to say bad things about Bob Lemon. I did what?

Bob Lemon asked me to join the team that season. I wanted to go home. I sat in the press box because that's where I was supposed to sit. I didn't say anything to sportswriters. Those sportswriters were Bob Lemon's guys.

For a guy who would eventually manage, I don't think Lou had the greatest understanding of the game. There was a night in Minnesota when Amos Otis was the designated hitter, and we were up by just a run. I wanted Otis—my best defensive outfielder—in the game. Of course, that meant our pitcher would have to hit. Well, the Twins tied it up, and Piniella made the last out in the top of the 12th inning. I was bringing in a new pitcher, and I needed to make a double switch. So I took Piniella out of the game.

Lou didn't understand. He thought I was taking him out because of his defense. He tore up the clubhouse. After the game, one of my guys came to me and said, "Hey, Lou's pretty hot."

I went to him and said, "What's your problem?" He said he couldn't believe I took him out for defense. I explained that I hadn't taken him out for defense, that I just didn't want our pitcher hitting in the next few innings. But he had no clue.

One night in Texas, I wanted to let some of the extra guys play. We were gonna play a doubleheader that night, so I was gonna let Kurt Bevacqua, one of my bench guys, play left field for Piniella in the first game and third base for Paul Schaal in the second game.

Now, you've gotta know Bevacqua. He's a clown.

I'd already made out my lineup, but Bevacqua, who hadn't seen the lineup yet, came walking by my office and said sarcastically, "Where am I playing today, Skip?"

I was gonna play along, so I said, "How about left field?"

"Great," he said.

A few minutes later, Bevacqua saw his name on the lineup card. For left field. He went around the clubhouse saying, "Hey, I just told the skipper I wanted to play left field today, and I'm in there. Ha! Ha!"

Piniella went nuts. Maybe I should've told Lou he was getting some rest, but he was a big boy. Instead, he whined.

The second game, I put Lou back in the lineup, but he came up and said, "Can't play. I've got a sore throat."

We won both games anyway.

That night on the plane home, Gib Twyman of the *Kansas City Star* came up and said he was writing a story on Piniella the next day. He said Piniella had bad-mouthed me. He said Piniella didn't think he was playing enough and wanted to be traded.

Well, a quick look at the stats showed that Piniella had played 79 of the first 81 games. But he was ripping me for keeping him out of the lineup. Fine, I said.

Again, I had no help from the front office or the media. Tallis was still against me. He resisted my evaluations, resisted my trade ideas, and so on. And it didn't help when he gave Piniella his money back after I had fined him. He did the same thing with Hal McRae. One night, I pinch hit for McRae because he was struggling. Hal went out in the runway and tore his uniform shirt off, so I fined him $100.

Tallis gave him his money back.

Cedric didn't really run a bad operation. It's just that he wasn't involved in the baseball side. I'd go up to his office to shoot the breeze, the same way other managers have done with me. But as soon as I'd start talking about trades, he'd pull out his golf putter and start tapping balls around the room. He'd say, "I learned something the other day from my golf pro. He says my hands are in the wrong place."

No, his head was.

That whole season, we were neck and neck with the A's. We really needed another starter, and Pat Dobson of Atlanta was available. The Braves wanted Norm Angelini and Al Autry, two of our young prospects. I'd had these kids at Triple A, and I knew they weren't championship players. I told Cedric to trade them.

Well, Cedric discussed it with Lou Gorman, the farm director, and they decided they "couldn't mortgage the future for the present." So we didn't get Pat Dobson, and he got traded to the Yankees instead. He went 9–8 in New York, and he even beat us one night on a two-hit shutout. After the game, some writers asked, "Wouldn't you have liked to have had Dobson?" And I blew up. I said we could've had him if we'd gotten off our tails, if our front office took Geritol.

The next day, it was all blown up in the papers: "GM And Manager Feuding!" Cedric called me in for a meeting and said, "Jack, don't worry. You don't have to win the pennant your first year as a big-league manager."

"What do you mean?" I said. "You win the pennant when you can win the pennant. You don't pick the year you win it."

The last day of the season, Cedric called me in for

another meeting. He wanted to talk money. He said I'd done a wonderful job, but that he could only offer me a small raise. Well, I'd made $30,000 my first year, and I was hoping I'd get $40,000 or maybe $35,000. Cedric offered me $32,000.

I sort of blew my top. I said, "How can you stand there and say I did a good job and give me a $2,000 raise?" A week before, he'd told me he was gonna give some mediocre rookie a $20,000 raise. But I was getting $2,000?

I said, "You must not think I did very well." I told him I was leaving, and if he didn't think I'd tell him to take this job and stick it, he was wrong.

I drove back to North Carolina, and when I arrived, Carol said Cedric had called six or seven times. He wanted me to call him back. I told her he'd have to wait until morning.

When I did call him, he was offering me $35,000. What the hell. I took it.

Thing was, Ewing Kauffman was great to me. He called me to say he wished he could've given me more money, but 1973 was a rough year, with the recession and all. Just before Christmas, though, Kauffman sent me 100 shares of stock in his own development company. Now it's worth 2,200 shares. I appreciated that.

The battle lines had definitely been drawn. It was Kauffman, myself, and Syd Thrift on one side, and Tallis and Gorman on the other. See, it all started when I was still managing the Triple-A club. Kauffman had this idea to open a baseball academy, where we'd go and find the best athletes in the country and teach them to play baseball. Thrift, now the Pittsburgh Pirate general manager, was in charge of putting it together. I thought it was a great idea.

There were so many kids from poor areas who never got to play much baseball. Syd would hold tryout camps and find the kids. He figured he couldn't teach them how to throw and hit, but he could spot good hand-eye coordination.

On the other hand, Tallis and Gorman thought it was undermining their farm system. They refused to see that this was really just a supplement to their farm system.

In addition to managing the Triple-A club, I was running their instructional-league program as well. I saw what Syd was doing, and it was great. One day, Mr. Kauffman asked me if we had any prospects in the academy, and I said yes. He asked for a scouting report, and I went on to list Frank White, Ron Washington, Sheldon Mallory, and a few others as prospects.

When Kauffman mentioned my findings to Tallis and Gorman, Gorman called me and said, "Jack, don't you ever lie to Mr. Kauffman again."

"Lie?"

"Yes, lie. You told him there were prospects in the academy."

"Damn right," I said. "There are prospects."

"My scouts say there aren't," Gorman said.

I went on to tell him that if he didn't want my opinion not to ask me. And I told him if he wanted someone else to run his instructional league, that was fine, too. Maybe he could find someone who'd tell him what he wanted to hear.

Anyway, I was really high on Frank White, an infielder who you've heard of by now. But Gorman and Tallis held a vendetta against White because he was from the academy. They were determined to keep him down, saying he wasn't a prospect. I'd keep trying to get him on my Triple-A team, and they wouldn't give him to me. So when I became the Royals' manager, I brought him to spring training. He was a shortstop and a second baseman, and he had a hell of a spring. We had Freddie Patek as our regular shortstop, and we had Cookie Rojas as our regular second baseman. I figured Rojas was nearing the end of his career, so I sent White down to Triple A and had him play second base.

The regular season began, and we were in third place when Patek got hurt and went on the 15-day disabled list. Cedric asked who I wanted to bring up: "Do you want Jose Arcia or Cal Meyer?"

"Neither," I said. "I know those guys, and they can't help me." I told him I wanted Frank White.

"He's not ready yet," Tallis said. "So who do you want?"

I kept telling Cedric that Frank White was the best player for us, and he kept telling me to decide who I wanted by the next morning.

The next morning, he called and asked, "Arcia or Meyer?"

I said if he didn't give me Frank White I was gonna go with 24 players. Cedric finally relented, and he gave me White.

In Frank's first game, he got two hits off Jim Palmer, the Cy Young Award winner.

In Cleveland a few days later, he got three hits off Gaylord Perry.

In Anaheim, he hit a line drive off Nolan Ryan that almost took Ryan's head off.

Our club went from third place to first. Patek came back, and I had to send White down. And Cedric was still saying he was a good utility player and nothing more.

By 1975, I had Frank on my club for good. Cookie

Rojas had lost a lot of range by that time, and I talked to Joe Burke (who had replaced Tallis) about making White the everyday second baseman.

"Oh, Jack," Burke said. "The fans are on you bad enough. Cookie's popular. If you take him out, they'll be all over you."

I said, "What is this? A popularity contest? Aren't we supposed to win?"

Burke said, "Let's wait until the end of the year. We'll give Cookie a big appreciation night."

Well, in the meantime, I got fired and replaced by Whitey Herzog. And the first thing Whitey did was put Frank White at second base.

Tallis, for one, used to resist all change. After our first season—when we finished in second place in 1973—I thought we needed a much deeper bench. We'd just gotten Hal McRae the year before, and that wasn't enough. Hell, Cedric wanted to trade McRae after 1973, and I talked him out of it.

What we really needed was some better catching and pitching. During the '73 World Series, we began talking to the Yankees, who were interested in our big first baseman, John Mayberry, and our shortstop, Patek. Mayberry had just had a big year and he had a lot of market value.

Well, I really wanted reliever Sparky Lyle. I kept throwing his name out, and the Yankees kept saying no. But we finally came up with a helluva package: we'd trade Mayberry and Patek to the Yankees for catcher Thurmon Munson, first baseman Chris Chambliss, shortstop Jimmy Mason, outfielder Bobby Murcer, and two young minor-league pitchers, Scott McGregor and Tippy Martinez.

Unbelievable. We would've won the pennant the next three years.

Cedric said, "Jack, what do you know about these

young pitchers? What makes you think they're so good? They're Double-A, Triple-A pitchers.''

I said, "Cedric, they can pitch. Trust me.''

Cedric said he couldn't trade Mayberry. He said he'd get run out of town. Popularity contests. So it fell through.

I knew we needed bench strength, and it showed in 1974 when both Mayberry and Otis went down with major injuries. We finished fifth, and I was blamed. All of a sudden, I was a lousy manager.

Undermining. In 1973, I wanted to pick up Deron Johnson in a trade from Philadelphia. I told Cedric, who said he'd send one of his scouts in to see Johnson. His scout said Johnson was through, but I called my man, Syd Thrift, and asked him if he'd go and see Johnson, too. Syd liked Johnson and said he could still play.

Cedric did nothing.

A few days later, Johnson got traded to the A's— our division rival—for some worthless minor leaguer. I said, "Gee whiz, Cedric. How could we let that happen?''

He said the deal had already been struck with the A's when we inquired about Johnson. And I believed him. But at the winter meetings later that year, I was talking to Paul Owens of the Phillies, who said Cedric never called him about Deron Johnson. Unbelievable.

Bottom line was that there was just too much friction for me in Kansas City. The whole Charlie Lau thing was a real mess, too. Charlie, who died in 1984, was our batting coach, and it was quite clear he wanted my job. He'd go behind my back and create a group of his own players who'd do everything he said. I truly believe he fed them lies about me. Undermining.

We had a rule that there would be no alcohol on team flights, but Charlie would bring it on anyway and give it to his clique of 10 or 12 players. Guys like Patek and Buck Martinez and McRae and George Brett.

Charlie tried turning Brett against me. At that time, Brett was just a kid, fresh up from Omaha. And Charlie told Brett I resisted bringing him up, which was a lie. What happened was that Brett got hot at Omaha, and the people there recommended that we bring him up. Cedric and Lou Gorman were thinking about doing it, but I'd known from past experience that Cedric didn't always get objective reports. I'd seen Brett in spring training and knew he had a great future, and I was willing to bring him up. But I said to Cedric, "Why don't you let Charlie Lau go down and look at him, and I'll have Syd Thrift (who was also our advance scout) look at him also."

Syd came back from Omaha raving about Brett and a pitcher named Steve Mingori. That's all I needed to hear. But somehow the story got twisted around that I didn't want Brett. It just wasn't so.

Charlie was also undermining my pitching coach, Galen Cisco. He'd pull pitchers into the film room and say, "I discovered what you're doing wrong." I felt it was getting to be too much of a problem, so I decided to get rid of Charlie. I had what I felt was a confidential meeting with Cedric. We were gonna replace Lau with Steve Boros, who later managed the A's and the Padres.

But three days before the '74 season ended, Lau approached me and asked what was going on. He said, "I understand you're thinking about making a change."

I guess Tallis had told him. See, he was Tallis's

guy. But I was up front with Charlie. I told him there was too much friction and a change was necessary. Some players balked at it, but it was something we had to do.

If it wasn't one thing, it was another. The media was all over me, too. Bill Beck, who was then the travelling secretary, told me that several writers used to sit in the press box and vow to get me fired. It all stemmed back to the Bob Lemon thing, I suppose.

In 1975, it reached its peak. The newspapers were all negative, and yet we were 50–46 and in second place when I got fired. Joe Burke broke the news to me on the way back from Milwaukee. He said it was a PR move, that he didn't want to make the change and that I was the best manager he'd ever worked with.

"But," Joe said, "the fans are all over you."

I figured the Royals were just a year away from winning. I really felt 1976 would be our year. And they did win the division in 1976.

Under Herzog.

At the 1980 World Series in Kansas City, I ran into Gib Twyman of the *Kansas City Star*. Gib said he'd had something on his mind for five years. When I managed the Royals, he said, he'd gone out of his way to make me look bad. And now he was apologizing. He said that now that he was a born-again Christian, he had to tell me he was sorry.

I told him, "It all worked out for the best. I'm with the Padres, and it's a better job."

Still, I was relieved in a way. I always knew the press hadn't treated me fairly in Kansas City, and it was good to hear it from the horse's mouth.

But not all my memories of Kansas City are bad ones. During my first season, the good people of South Amboy—my hometown—gave me a "Jack

McKeon Day" at Yankee Stadium. About 6,000 people drove the 25 miles from South Amboy, including
my mother and my sisters. The only sad thing about
it was that my dad had died and couldn't be there. He
had encouraged me so much, and his dream had
always been for me to play or manage in the big
leagues. Still, I remember standing there at Yankee
Stadium, knowing he was watching me. That was
enough to satisfy me. That was enough.

Also that year, Joe Garagiola had his own national TV show, and he did a feature on me. He
called it, "The Life of a Rookie Manager." Hell, he
and his cameras followed me everywhere. We were in
New York, walking down Seventh Avenue, and Joe
was stopping people on the street. He'd say, "Sir, do
you know who this is? This is Jack McKeon, the new
manager of the Kansas City Royals." And the guy
would run away.

One time, he stopped a hippie. The guy had a
scraggly beard and was wearing a beat-up army coat,
and Joe told him, "Hey, I'd like you to meet Jack
McKeon, who grew up nearby in South Amboy, New
Jersey. He's now the manager of the Kansas City
Royals."

"So what," the hippie said.

The cameras even followed me onto the team bus,
but my players were hooting and hollering and
swearing so loud that they couldn't use the tape on
TV. In the end, though, it turned out to be a decent
show.

Joe once interviewed my son, Kelly, on his syndi-
cated radio show. Joe was fascinated that Kelly, at age
12, chewed tobacco.

"How long have you been chewing, Kelly?" Joe
asked him on the air.

"Five or six years," Kelly said.

"Don't you think it's bad for you?" Joe asked.

"Well, I've cut down on it this year," Kelly said. "It's pretty tough to chew now that I've got braces."

"Oh," Joe said.

Speaking of chewing, there was the time I had the spitting contest with Doc Severinson, the musician from the Tonight Show. He was in Kansas City for a summer-stock theater performance, and someone brought him on the field before one of our games.

He saw me chewing tobacco, and he got this gleam in his eye. "Gimme a chew," he said.

I gave him a chew.

"Let's have a spitting contest," he said.

So I chuckled. I'd been chewing for 30 years. How was some TV personality gonna outdo me?

What I forgot was you've gotta have strong lips to play a trumpet. We put a couple of pebbles a few feet away from us, and Doc was spitting line drives. He was hitting his pebble every time.

Me, I was spraying my shots. I have this gap in my teeth, so that didn't help.

I guess he was the unofficial winner. He went back on "The Tonight Show," bragging about how he'd defeated Jack McKeon, the Kansas City manager, in a spitting contest. He mentioned it three shows in a row. Hell, I was getting calls from all over the country.

But, yeah, I was a big chewer. Everyone knew it. I'd get spittoons for Christmas and birthday presents all the time. I didn't know what to do with all of them. They do make lovely flower pots.

When Royals Stadium opened, I had a problem. It was so clean and beautiful. I mean, you usually just spit on the field. But I wasn't sure if you could spit on that artificial turf. So I did. In fact, I was the first person to spit tobacco juice in the home dugout at

Royals Stadium. George Toma, the groundskeeper, came running over in hysterics.

"Jack, Jack," he screamed. "Don't do that. It was all so clean."

The next day, George showed up with a couple of pails for me to spit in.

By and large, I had a good relationship with the Royal players. Pitcher Paul Splittorff is one of my favorite people in baseball. If you told him to do 20 sprints from the left-field line to the right-field line, he'd do it. And he wouldn't cheat and forget to touch the line. He was disciplined.

I had him in Omaha one year, and the Royals called to say they needed a lefty. I had Tom Burgmeier and Splittorff, and I told them to take Burgmeier. I just didn't think Paul was ready. But I didn't know that Charlie Metro—the Royal manager the year before—had promised Paul that he'd be the first pitcher up from the minors. So when I sent Burgmeier up, Paul was a little disgusted. I don't blame him.

The next year, he was sent to me again at Omaha, and he was really struggling. I told him not to worry. He was working on a change-up and a curveball, and he was polishing his slider. I knew he'd be ready for the big leagues in about four weeks.

Well, about six or seven weeks later, Cedric called me and wanted a pitcher named Lance Clemens. I said Lance wasn't ready, but Paul Splittorff was. Cedric said his staff didn't like Splittorff, so I told him to send his scouts down to Omaha. I'd have Splittorff start one game and Clemens start the next. Sure enough, Splittorff pitched a 1-0 shutout, and Clemens got bombed. Splittorff got called up and struck out 12 White Sox in his debut.

Splittorff reminded me a lot of Jim Kaat, who I'd

had at Missoula. Kaat was only 17 at the time, but you just knew he would pitch in the big leagues. I remember Calvin Griffith, the Twins owner, had come to Missoula with Joe Haynes, his vice president, and they'd seen Kaat pitch a three-hitter. Haynes said he didn't think Kaat had the stuff to pitch in the big leagues, but I told him that Jim made up for it with brains and savvy. I bet him two steak dinners that Kaat would be in the big leagues within two years. Six months later, Kaat was in the big leagues.

Some of my other favorite Royals were Amos Otis and Tony Solaita and Harmon Killebrew, whom we picked up near the end of his career.

Amos, I remember, had been fined by Bob Lemon in 1972 for not hustling. When I took over, I sat him down and said I'd be up front with him. If I thought he was dogging it, I'd tell him. But he didn't dog it at all. Then one night in Cleveland, he failed to run out three ground-ball outs. I saw him around the batting cage the next day and said, "How's the leg?"

"Fine," he said. "What do ya mean?"

I said, "Amos, I don't think you ran those balls out."

"You're kidding, Skip," he said.

Well, that night he busted his rear end down the first-base line. Amos wasn't a loafer. It's just that sometimes you hit a ball right at somebody and you're frustrated. He was a good kid.

Tony Solaita was a big Samoan, with great power. I'd had him in 1968 when I managed a co-op team in High Point, North Carolina, right before I started with the Royals. He hit 51 homers for me. So in 1974, I signed him for the Royals. Another great kid.

The thing I learned when I managed the Royals

was that you gotta be part manager, part psychiatrist. Shortstop Freddie Patek was an example. Every time he'd get wiped out at second base, he'd just lie there motionless. It was sickening. He was a hell of an actor.

I'll never forget the day my trainer, Jim Dudley, got him back for always crying wolf. One day, Patek came in the trainer's room complaining of another sore back and said, "Duds, I'm stiff. I need a rubdown."

Duds—looking dead serious—said, "Wait a minute, Freddie. I'll grab my coat and go downtown with you. We'll both get one."

One day, Freddie was in a really bad batting slump, and we were leaving on a Monday for a California swing. After Sunday's game, he came into my office and said he was quitting baseball. He said he had found religion and was gonna retire. I wished him well and I told him I'd really enjoyed managing him.

Then I said, "Hey, Freddie, if you change your mind, the bus leaves tomorrow morning at 11."

He was on the bus.

Well, when I got fired, a bunch of guys came over to my house in Independence, Missouri, to wish me well. Hell, we partied for three days.

Actually, it hit my kids the hardest. They had become sort of minor celebrities in school, and I remember my little daughter Kori saying, "Dad, you gotta get another job so we can be popular again."

The phone rang. "McKeon? It's Finley . . .
Consider the squeeze." Boom. He hung up.

10
"McKeon? It's Finley!"
(Who Else?)

WHEN THE ROYALS said goodbye at last, Carol and the kids and I drove home to North Carolina. I sat around like a bump on a log, which—as you know— isn't like me at all.

Carol, who preferred me yelling at umpires and not at the kids, said, "Jack, why don't you do something? Get out of the house."

If it wasn't an umpire kicking me out, it was my wife.

No, really, she was making a lot of sense. I needed something to do. Fortunately, I got a call that August of 1975 from Charlie Finley, that eccentric owner of the Oakland A's. It was the first of many, *many* calls from Charlie Finley. But I'm getting ahead of myself.

Charlie needed a favor. The A's were headed for the playoffs, and he needed me as an advance scout, someone to go in and check out the competition. I told Charlie the Royals were still paying me, but I'd be glad to work for expenses only. He didn't seem like a bad guy. I said I'd give him a hand.

Then, I spent the winter managing in Puerto Rico. Charlie had thanked me for a job well done, and that was that. I never thought about the guy again.

By the end of the winter, I had another job. The Atlanta Braves had called me and asked if I'd manage their Triple-A club in Richmond for 1976. I wanted to manage again in the major leagues, so I thought this could be a stepping-stone, and I took the job.

I had this young catcher named Dale Murphy. He had started the year in Double A and had trouble with his throwing arm. I mean, he could throw the ball 100 mph, but he couldn't throw it in the vicinity of second base on stolen-base attempts. The Braves tried working with him (they'd have him throw at spare tires), but he was a sensitive kid and began trying too hard. That's when I got ahold of him.

He was letting his defense disturb his offense, too. The kid needed to tone it down. The fans started booing him (yes, it's true, they booed the Murph), so I got him out of there. I benched him. I wasn't gonna bury him.

Some major-league farm director came to watch us play one day. He'd come to see Murphy, and he saw him all right—on the bench.

"You got Murphy, don't you, Jack?" the farm director said to me after the game.

"Yep."

"Well, how the hell can you bench this kid," the guy said. "He's a top prospect."

I lost it. I said, "Let me tell you something, you pencil-pushing SOB. He's a great prospect, and I want to keep it that way. There's a time when you back off and wait for the right time. This ain't the right time."

The right time came against Memphis. We were in the 14th inning, and we trailed by two runs. We had two men on, and I sent Murphy to pinch hit.

Memphis brought in a right-hander to face him. The count got to 2 and 2; then Murph crushed one over the center-field fence. Suddenly, he was a hero again. They had been ready to lynch the poor kid, but then he was on a tear—eight home runs in eight days. He carried us the rest of the season, and he's gone on to have a pretty good life.

I'm not saying I'm some genius. I'm just saying you gotta have gut feelings inside your gut.

The following year, 1977, Braves' owner Ted Turner wanted me to be his assistant. Basically, he wanted me for my gut feelings. I'd help advise him on trades and so forth. I appreciated the offer, and I told him so. But I really wanted to manage again, and that's when I heard the crazy news about Chuck Tanner. Charlie Finely—that man again—had traded Tanner, his manager, to Pittsburgh for catcher Manny Sanguillen and something like $100,000. Tanner had been under contract to Finley, and since the Pirates really wanted Tanner, Finley wasn't about to give him away for free.

Well, I immediately called Finley to tell him I wanted Tanner's job. Fortunately, I was already on his list, and he later flew me in for dinner and a chat. We got back to his office and he offered me the job. Took me a couple seconds to say yes.

We talked money. He asked, "What do ya think ya should make, Jack?"

I hadn't heard that question before—especially not

in Kansas City—but I'm no hog. I said I'd made $40,000 my final year with the Royals and I didn't know what to ask for. He said, "Fine, how about $45,000?"

I nodded.

So we began talking about a coaching staff, and I wanted my old friend Lee Stange as my pitching coach. Charlie said fine. He wanted Red Schoendienst as his first-base coach, and I said fine.

He went to call Red right away. He dialed the number, but the phone was busy.

"Busy, busy, busy," Charlie was grimacing. "I hate busy signals."

I was getting my first real glimpse of Charlie O.

He dialed the operator. "Hello! This is Dr. Finley! It's an emergency, and I've got to get through to Mr. Red Schoendienst. Will you please interrupt his call and say, 'Dr. Finley's on the line. It's an emergency.' "

The operator put him through. "Red! This is Charlie! . . . Charlie Finley! Come be my first-base coach! . . . You can? . . . Great!"

Boom. He slammed the phone.

Now, he gave me some ground rules. "Jack, you're my manager," he said, "but don't ever forget that I'm in charge. Whether you agree or disagree, I not only own the club, but I'm the general manager as well."

I nodded.

So I left his office and called Ted Turner to tell him I wouldn't be needing his job after all. He sounded alarmed: "Jack, you took that job? You're crazy! You'll get fired out there."

"I know, Ted," I said.

"Well, when you get fired," he said, "give me a call and I'll have a job for you."

"Thanks Ted," I said.

So Charlie called an elaborate press conference to announce my hiring. He told me exactly what to do. He wanted me to say, "Well, folks, the only reason Charlie hired me was so that he could trade me to some other team for a player and $200,000, not $100,000."

Everyone thought that was kinda funny.

Spring training began, and everything was normal until Charlie called me to tell me about his "Magic Water." It seemed he was sending down some pasteurized water for the entire team, and I was supposed to call a press conference. He told me to deliver the following speech: "All our guys will be drinking Magic Water this season. It really works. Just look at Charlie. He drinks it, and he's the fountain of youth. This water will make us play 10 times better."

So that's what I said at the press conference.

Everyone thought it was kinda funny.

Later in the season, we lost a close game, and Charlie screamed, "I know why we lost! We ran out of Magic Water!"

Really, I never had a problem with Charlie, even though he'd call anywhere from two to twelve times a day. I decided always to leave word where I was, because he'd find me anyway. He'd find me at restaurants, he'd find me at my brother's house, he'd find me sitting on the toilet. You name it. Some people bad-mouthed him, but I figured it was great to be working for a guy who cared. He was an idea man. He was the one who implemented different-colored home uniforms, designated runners, World Series night games, orange baseballs, and so on. Gotta hand it to him.

We talked about many subjects, and especially

about trades. I'd call him and he'd answer, "Hello,
Finley's Packing House. Cattle for sale or trade. Can
I help you?"

He'd call every morning at six or so. He'd disguise
his voice: "Good morning, sir! This is your friendly
wake-up call and your friendly wake-up man!"

Other times, it was "McKeon! Are you in bed?"

"Yeah, Charlie."

"Jack, don't you know only whores make money in
bed? Get up, get up! Be like Charlie! Get going!"

Charlie took Geritol, I'm telling you.

Dick Allen always used to complain to me, and I
remember Charlie waking me up one morning to
say, "Hello! Good morning, sir. Is this the team psy-
chologist? How are you working out with your
patients?"

With Allen, I had no patience. It was late in Dick's
career when Charlie contemplated signing him. He
had asked me what I thought of Allen, and I said
Dick Allen was a hell of a player and could help any
team, if he wanted to play badly enough.

Charlie decided to have Allen over for dinner that
night. They were gonna eat Charlie's famous home-
made chili. The next day, Charlie called to say, "I
think I'll sign that Allen guy. He likes my chili."

So he scheduled a press conference. I was supposed
to pick Dick up at the hotel at 7:30 A.M. for a 10 A.M.
announcement, but when I got there, Dick yawned
and said, "I don't want a press conference."

Charlie would have blown his top, so I sold Dick
on the idea. I told him all the ladies in town would
be watching on TV or something like that. He
agreed to go.

So we assembled at a hotel, and I gave my spiel on
how happy we were to have a guy like Dick Allen.

Dick took his turn to speak, and he thanked the Lord for giving him another opportunity to play and he said his batting average was in the hands of the Lord, too.

Reporters began pumping questions at him.

"Dick, what's it gonna be? Designated hitter or first base?"

He looked over at me, and said, "I'll do whatever the man wants."

That was nice. So in our season opener, I put Dick at first base. The next day—a doubleheader—I put Dick at first base in the first game and at DH in the second game.

Dick got angry.

"I'm not playing DH!" he said. "I have a deal with Charlie. I don't have to DH!"

Well, maybe I'd misunderstood him at the press conference. Dick had said he'd do "whatever the man wants," but now I wasn't sure which man he meant. So I pinch hit for him in the first inning.

I asked Charlie about it afterward.

"Well, Jack, maybe I did make a deal with him," Charlie said.

So I never DH'ed him again.

Listen, Charlie didn't consult me about everything. A lot of times he'd just show up on the road to deliver invigorating pep talks to the team. He thought he was Knute Rockne, he really did. Also, he and Bear Bryant had been personal friends. Charlie would fly down for Alabama football games and sit in on the Bear's halftime speeches.

So he came into the clubhouse in Anaheim one day and called everyone into the room. All eyes were on him. There was silence. He began pacing. Just what Rockne used to do.

Suddenly, he looked up. "Listen!" he said. "I personally signed you, you, you, and you! . . . Well, what's wrong with you guys?!"

He was angry that we'd stranded some baserunners the night before.

"When opportunity knocks," he said, "you've got to be able to take advantage! You have to take care of Mr. Opportunity!"

Now he ran to the other end of the clubhouse. He put his ear close to the door. He pounded on the door three times—to make it seem like someone was knocking—and held the following conversation with himself.

"Who's there?"

"Mr. Opportunity!"

"Oh, hello Mr. Opportunity. Mr. Opportunity, C'mooooooooooooon in!"

And he whipped the door open.

Nobody came in, of course, and nobody kept a straight face, of course.

We went out and lost.

By the way, in that same pep talk, he had spoken about desire and determination. He'd point to his head and say, "This is determination, boys." And then he'd point to his heart and say, "This is desire, boys." He wanted to see if everyone understood, so he pointed to his heart again and asked one of the players, "What's this, son?"

"The bunt!" said the player.

For the next few days, everyone was walking around pointing to their heads and their hearts. "What's this?" one guy would ask. "The take sign," another would answer. "What's this?" another would ask. "The squeeze," another would answer.

The guys preferred not to play in Chicago because that's where Charlie lived. Inevitably, he'd waltz in

I've worked with a lot of "dummies" before, but this one, sent to
help me coach third base, was ridiculous.

Billy Martin and I had the honor of having our picture taken with the bat boy.

This is the infamous Spoonie, a.k.a. Chuck Weatherspoon. He wouldn't sit for the picture until we promised there were no snakes or ghosts hiding behind the camera.

There was just too much friction for me in Kansas City, between
Lou Piniella blaming me because he had a bad season and
Charlie Lau trying to turn my players against me.

The only thing missing in this picture is the telephone Charlie Finley called me on 20 times a day.

The San Diego Padres present their new general manager to the media in 1979.

The 1984 Padres' parade to Jack Murphy Stadium to celebrate our pennant. For Carol and me, it was the highlight of 20 years in baseball.

Benito Santiago was the 1987 National
League Rookie of the Year, and I'm
convinced it will be the first of many awards
for him.

As a manager, Larry Bowa quickly became notorious for his
temper, but no one can argue that he's not a fierce competitor
and a strong leader.

The 1987 major-league batting champion, Tony Gwynn, is a true star; he's a hard worker who gets the most out of his tremendous ability. Someone should tell him, though, that you're supposed to unwrap the cigar.

with a speech or some advice for our hitters. One day, he decided to let us know how to hit Wilbur Wood of the White Sox, who had a great knuckleball. He walked in and had someone fetch him a little-league bat.

"Do you know what this is?" he said, holding the bat with both hands.

Silence.

"This," he said, "is a little-league bat. And why is this so small? Because little leaguers can't handle the big bat. And that's what I'm trying to say here, gentlemen. You have better bat control if you choke up on the bat. That's why little leaguers have small bats."

Silence.

"Now, Wilbur Wood is pitching tonight, gentlemen. I've been watching his last few starts, and I'll tell you how to hit him. Get up there and choke up! And move up real far in that batter's box so you can hit that knuckler before it knuckles!"

Silence.

The guys went out and got five runs in the first inning. But nobody choked up and nobody moved up in the batter's box.

The next night, Charlie strolled in with a smile.

"Listen guys, Stan Bahnsen is pitching tonight, so let me tell you how to hit him . . ."

Charlie certainly liked the idea of choking up on the bat. One Monday night, we were playing a nationally televised game against the Yankees, back when Ron Guidry was the best pitcher in baseball. Guidry had us helpless that night. He was throwing a one-hitter or something in the seventh inning. Charlie was watching on TV back in Chicago and gave me a call in the dugout.

"McKeon? It's Finley."

"Hi, Charlie."

"Listen, Jack. Tell those hitters to choke up, choke up."

"They are, Charlie."

"God damnit," he screamed, "they are not! I'm watching on TV. They are not!"

"Ok, I'll tell them."

So my first hitter the next inning was Miguel Dilone. I pulled him aside and said, "Look, I want you to choke up all the way to the label. I want you to really overdo it. Charlie's watching. Make damn sure he can't say you weren't choking up. Take a strike and then go back to normal."

Miguel nodded. When he went up there, he choked up about 30 inches.

Charlie didn't call back.

Listen, we had a bunch of .220 and .225 hitters, so we weren't gonna hit much anyway. But he'd always call and say, "Tell 'em to choke up, choke up, choke up."

And boom. He'd hang up.

He'd call the dugout six to eight times a week. It got so every time the phone rang, the players would start chirping, "Choke up, choke up, choke up," before I even answered.

Listen, I never minded. As I've said, a lot of owners wouldn't take the time to be involved. Charlie cared. And I wasn't one of those managers who spent off-days at the golf course. I spent my time talking baseball, to anyone who wanted to. Charlie included.

He'd leave word for me to call him, and when I did, he'd answer, "This is the law! Identify yourself and start talking!"

One day, he jabbed me in the ribs and said, "Jack, I'm intrigued with speed in baseball. In fact, you may call me 'Speed' if you want to."

Next time I called him, I said, "Hello, Speed. How's everything going?" He burst out laughing.

In truth, Charlie thought speed was the key to winning. He'd say, "Jack, we've got to use our rabbits. We've got too many trucks." To Charlie, anyone who couldn't run the 100 in 9.7 seconds was a truck. He once flew into Minnesota to surprise us with another pep talk. We were in second or third place, and Charlie thought the guys needed some extra confidence.

"We're gonna steal the pennant, men," he told them. "We're not gonna win it, we're gonna steal it."

That night, we had two guys picked off first base. He came in afterward and said, "We can still steal the pennant, men, despite your manager and coaches!"

See, Charlie thought it was our fault whenever guys got picked off. He thought it was also our fault when a guy got thrown out at the plate.

I felt especially sad for Red Schoendienst, our third-base coach, who really caught a lot of grief from Charlie. One night, Glenn Burke was on third with one out. We had a one-run lead, and there was a short fly ball to left. Burke faked tagging up and stayed put. But the throw from the outfield got past the catcher—Burke would've been safe if he'd gone. We ended up losing, 3–2, and Charlie came downstairs and blamed it all on Red.

"Get all the coaches in your office!" he hollered at me.

When they all sat down, he glared at Red.

"Why didn't you send Burke?!" Charlie asked Red. Red said he had.

Charlie paused. "Well, Red. I've been watching you, and you need a little pizzazz coaching third! Put some life into it! Let me show you how!"

First, Charlie cleared all the chairs out of his way.
Then, he got in a crouched position and cupped his
hands around his mouth so his words would be
amplified.

"This is how you do it, Red! When the fly ball
goes up, you holler, 'Back! Back! Back! Back!' And
when it's caught, you run down the line with the
baserunner, hollering, 'Go! Go! Go! Go!' "

Red nodded.

A week later, Charlie moved Red from third base
to first base.

The new third-base coach was Bobby Hofman,
and he immediately met controversy, too. Larry
Lintz—one of our rabbits—was on first base in the
15th inning one night, and Hofman flashed the steal
sign. Lintz didn't run, so Hofman flashed it again.
Lintz still didn't run.

So Earl Williams hit into a double play on the next
pitch, and we ended up losing. I was hot, and I fined
Lintz $200. Lintz didn't appreciate it, of course, and
complained to Charlie.

Charlie called me up and said, "You fined Lintz,
huh?"

I said yes.

"Darnit Jack. That wasn't Lintz's fault. That was
your fault. Your coaches aren't giving the signs
clearly enough."

I was still hot. So I held a team meeting the next
day to make it real simple. I told the players that one
clap was the bunt, two claps was the steal, and three
claps was the hit and run.

I figured they could at least count.

Another of my third-base coaches, Cal Ermer, had
an episode one day, with outfielder Billy North.
North, who was on second base, tried scoring on a

single to center field, even though Ermer held him up. The throw was off line, and North scored, so nobody ever said a word about it.

Three days later, though, Charlie called me.

"McKeon? It's Finley! Listen, Jack, did North go through a stop sign the other night?"

"Yeah, but he was safe," I said.

"So what're you gonna do about it?" Charlie asked.

"Nothing," I said. "He was safe."

"Jack, you gotta fine him $250."

"Why?"

"Jack, if you're driving down a street and come to a four-way stop sign and you go through that stop sign and a policeman sees you, you have disobeyed the law! And pretty soon, you'll hear a *Awwwww-rurrrrr* (he was trying to make a siren sound). And that officer will pull you over and say, 'Mr. McKeon, you have disobeyed the law! I have to write you a ticket. You're gonna be fined $250 for disobeying.' Well, Jack, it's the same for Billy North. He broke the law."

"Charlie," I said, "that happened 3 or 4 days ago. I can't fine the guy now."

"That's OK," Charlie said, "provided you have a clubhouse meeting to explain the law. You tell them the policeman story, just the way I told you. You hear?"

So the next day, I told the guys to pay attention to their coaches and not to run through signs the way Billy North did. I told them it was the law, just like running a stop sign would be. When I got to the *Awwwww-rurrrrr* part, the guys thought I was a little kooky, but who cared what they thought, anyway.

Charlie, of course, made sure I told the story correctly. He called the clubhouse man to see if I had held a meeting, and the clubhouse guy told him about the *Awwwww-rurrrrr* part. Charlie was relieved.

In a nutshell, Charlie wanted an exciting, run-oriented team. He was always talking about trading trucks for rabbits. Rabbit was his favorite word.

Once, Charlie was real excited about a minor leaguer we had, a guy from Jersey City named Mike Woodward. Charlie said, "Jack, he's a rabbit! I'm gonna bring him up to the big leagues, and you must use him every day. But if you gotta put him in the field, put him at second base. That's the only place he can play. Hear me?"

I heard him.

So I had Dilone as my No. 1 rabbit, and I had Woodward as my No. 2 rabbit. I'd pinch run them whenever I could. When Woodward showed up for his first game, Charlie slapped me on the back and said, "Get him in there, Jack. I won't tell you how to use him, but just get him in there."

It was a close game. Wayne Gross—a truck—led off the seventh inning with a single, and, naturally, I told Woodward to pinch run. Woodward jumped up—just like a rabbit should—and stretched. In the meantime, the other team was making a pitching change, and Woodward decided to wait in the dugout while their pitcher warmed up.

Poor Charlie. He was sitting behind the first-base dugout and couldn't see Woodward. All he could see was Gross—the truck—still standing on first base.

All of a sudden, I heard his voice: "Rabbit! Rabbit! Rabbit! Rabbit!"

Another night, we were ahead of Cleveland, 3-2, in

the bottom of the eighth, and once again I pinch ran Woodward for our truck, Wayne Gross. And because I had no more reserve infielders, I had to insert Woodward at second base in the ninth and move my regular second baseman, Mike Edwards, to third. Remember, Charlie had me promise to use Woodward only at second.

Well, my pitcher got the first hitter out, but the next batter singled and the next batter walked. Runners were on first and second, and Johnny Grubb, a left-handed hitter, was up.

I brought in a lefty pitcher, Bob Lacey. I needed a double play, and I figured I'd better put my best double-play combination back together (shortstop Rob Picciolo and Edwards). So I told Woodward to move to third, and I put Edwards back at second. Well, on the first pitch, Grubb lined one down to third. Woodward—who couldn't have been more than 5′10″—leaped and snared it and doubled up the runner at second. We won.

Hell of a move, right?

At 6 A.M., the phone rang.

"McKeon? It's Finley . . . They're all laughing at you. Your players, the other team, the media. All of baseball is laughing at you."

"Uh, Charlie, what're they laughing at?"

"Jack," he said, "I'm trying to help you become a good manager. I told you not to play Woodward anywhere but second base, and you went ahead and put him at third, didn't you."

"Yeah, Charlie," I said. "For one pitch."

Silence.

See, Charlie had only seen the box score. He hadn't seen the game. And when he saw in the box score

that Woodward played third, he thought I'd disobeyed his law completely. So I explained the whole
situation.

He listened, paused, and snapped, "So I guess you
think you're a damn genius now."

Most of the time, I was better off complying with
the law. Charlie gave me certain rules, and he told
me to follow them to a T. When I didn't, I almost
always got burned. For instance, he had this rule
with Mitchell Page, our leftfielder. Whenever we
were ahead by two runs in the sixth inning, I was to
take Page out. Or if we were ahead by one run in the
seventh, I'd take him out. Page was a hell of a hitter,
but he was no Gold Glove.

But one night in Oakland when we were ahead,
4–2, after six innings, he was the second hitter in the
bottom of the seventh. I figured I'd leave him in for
one more.

The opposing team immediately loaded the bases.
Then, the next batter lined a ball—where else?—to
Page in left field. It was headed straight at him, and
all he had to do was stand there and stick out his
glove. But instead, he charged the ball, and it sailed
straight over his head. Three runs scored, and we
lost.

At 6 A.M., the phone rang.

"McKeon? It's Finley!"

"Hi, Charlie."

"Listen, Jack. I told you to get Page out of there
with two run leads in the sixth inning. I'm trying to
help you become a good manager."

"Charlie, I thought you said take him out with a
two-run lead in the SEVENTH inning." (Of course,
I knew it was the sixth, but I wasn't gonna tell him.)

"No, damnit!" he shouted.

"Gee, Charlie," I said, "I screwed up."

The same thing happened all over again in Cleveland one night. Charlie's other rule was that I get catcher Earl Williams out of any game in the seventh or eighth inning, seeing as how Williams was all hit, no catch.

But that night in Cleveland, Doc Medich was pitching a super game, and Earl was calling all the right pitches. We were up, 1–0, in the bottom of the ninth, and I stayed with Earl.

Inevitably, someone got on base, and the next guy tried sacrificing him to second. Medich's first pitch was way inside, bounced off Earl's glove, and rolled to the backstop. They tied it up, and we eventually lost.

That night, we flew from Cleveland to Detroit. I got into my hotel room at 3 A.M.

At 3:30 A.M., the phone rang.

"McKeon? It's Finley. I want to let you know one thing. This is Charlie Finley's team. Not Jack McKeon's team. Do you understand? If not, I'll get someone else who does. I told you to get damn Williams out of the game."

Another day, we were down, 2–1, to the Royals, but we had the bases loaded in the seventh with no outs. Whitey Herzog, the Royals manager, brought in Al Hrabosky, and I knew we'd score at least two or three runs. Hrabosky was wild, and he was sure to walk in a run or two.

As he was warming up, the phone rang.

"McKeon? It's Finley . . . Consider the squeeze."

Boom. He hung up.

He was back in Chicago, and must've been listening on the radio.

Well, I considered the squeeze—for a second—and

then sent my hitter, Jeff Newman, out there to swing away. The count got to 2 and 1, then 3 and 2, and Newman struck out swinging. Fine, I said. Joe Wallis, my next guy, would surely get a hit or walk. The count got to 2 and 0, but he struck out, too.

Fine, I said. Here came Mike Edwards. Hrabosky threw, and Edwards popped up his first pitch to the second baseman.

As Frank White, the Royal second baseman, was circling under it, the phone rang.

"Damnit! I told you to squeeze!"

Boom. He hung up.

So I figured I'd better try to accommodate him. There was a night in Seattle when he called me and said, "Jack, let's do something different tonight."

I held my breath.

He said, "Use Larry Murray as your lead-off man, Jack, and have him get hit by a pitch."

I said, "Charlie, how the hell am I gonna do that?"

He said, "We'll give him two new suits of clothes if he gets hit, OK?"

"OK, Charlie," I said.

He went on to explain that when Murray got on, we'd pinch run Dilone. Then, we'd use a sacrifice bunt to get Dilone to second. Then, on the first pitch, Dilone would steal third. Then, the next guy would hit a sacrifice fly. We'd be ahead, 1–0.

"Right, Charlie," I said.

When Murray got ready to hit, I told him, "Listen, just get on. I don't care how. Just get on."

He walked.

I pinch ran Dilone.

We bunted him to second.

On the first pitch, Dilone tried stealing third, and

he beat the tag. Unfortunately, the ump called him out.

The next guy flied to left, so everything would've worked perfectly had the third-base ump made the right call.

The dugout phone rang.

"McKeon? It's Finley. Hey, we tried, didn't we?"

I found out later that Charlie had been throwing a party that night back at his place in Chicago. They were all watching the game on TV, and he was telling the whole group every move I was gonna make. He got a charge out of doing things like that.

The thing I really remember was how he gave me rabbits, rabbits, and more rabbits. Almost our entire bench was made up of speed guys, rather than right-handed or left-handed power hitters. One time we were besieged by a bunch of injuries, and I had to use a rabbit named Matt Alexander as my everyday outfielder. Actually, Alexander was doing a pretty decent job, but Charlie became a little concerned one day and called me in Seattle.

"Jack, get out the bible," he said.

"Charlie, what?" I asked.

"Now!" he said. "Get out the bible. The baseball bible, damnit. *The Baseball Register.*"

"Oh," I said. "I thought you meant the *real* Bible."

Anyway, I got out my Baseball Register, and he told me to turn to page 222.

"Look," he said. "Jim Tyrone, who we haven't been using, has more career home runs than Alexander. Alexander has three career homers, but Tyrone has seven career home runs. See that, Jack? Let's go for power tonight! Let's use Tyrone instead of Alexander!"

Well, I didn't see much difference. Alexander was a

rabbit, and so was Tyrone. Seven home runs to three didn't tell me much, but Charlie was the boss. I put Tyrone in the game, and we won, 1-0.

At 6 A.M., the phone rang.

"McKeon? It's Finley!"

"Hi, Charlie."

"Listen, Jack. I didn't get a chance to see the score last night. How'd we do?"

"We won, 1-0, Charlie."

"Oh great," he said. "How'd we get our run?"

"Let's see," I said. "Dilone got on, and then Tyrone singled him home."

"Ohhhhhhhhh," he said. "Tyrone, huh? Tyrone knocked in the winning run, huh? Greeeeeeeeat move, skipper!"

Boom. He hung up.

Those 6 A.M. phone calls were charming, you know. One morning he called and said, "What happened in the sixth inning last night, Jack?" (We'd had a 4-2 lead and a runner on first. Our best hitter, Page, was up, and it was a bunt situation).

"Wait a minute, Jack," he said. "Don't answer me. I'll tell you what you were thinking. You were thinking you had Mitchell Page up, your best hitter, and you weren't thinking about a sacrifice. No, you were thinking about getting two runs. Weren't you now, Jack?"

"That's right, Charlie," I said.

He shouted, "That's exactly what I thought! Let me remind you of one thing, son. If you want to be a hog, you'll end up eating manure."

Whatever.

He'd be back in his Chicago office listening to almost every game on radio, but he'd also be tuned into the clubhouse gossip. He'd call the clubhouse guy to get the scoop. One night, I replaced Page for defensive purposes, just the way Charlie wanted it. We were up by two runs in the sixth, so Page came out of the game. Well, five minutes later, I got a call from Charlie, who asked, "Where's Page? I don't think he's in the dugout anymore."

I assumed Page was up changing shirts or something, but then Charlie told me he was taking a shower and was getting ready to leave.

The clubhouse guy had told him.

Well, how was I gonna manage a game and baby-sit, too? Point is, Charlie wanted to know anything and everything about the team.

Later, we acquired Doc Ellis, who—to say the least—did not take orders too well. We kept a daily pitching chart, and the previous day's starting pitcher usually was in charge of it. Doc, however, didn't appreciate that rule and set a match to the chart one day.

"This is what they can do with their pitching chart!" he said as it went up in flames.

At the time, I didn't know what Doc had done, and Charlie heard about it only because the radio announcer told him. Still, Charlie didn't trust me completely and wondered if I'd lied about it. So he called me in Detroit that night.

"McKeon? It's Finley!"

"Hi, Charlie."

"Jack," he said, "I've been wondering. Do we keep charts on pitchers? And if so, how does it work?"

I told him the policy.

"Jack," he said, "Do you think we'd have a chart from tonight's game?"

I told him yes. And I told him that Lee Stange would have it.

Boom. He hung up.

So he called Stange and asked about the chart. Stange told him Ellis had burned it, and Charlie asked, "Lee, does Jack know about this?"

"No, not as far as I know," Stange said.

Boom. Charlie hung up. This was just his way of checking up on me.

Well, to say the least, we weren't the greatest team in 1977, even with the Magic Water. Just before I arrived in Oakland, Charlie had been wiped out by free agency. He'd lost Reggie Jackson and Bert Campanaris and Rollie Fingers and Gene Tenace. He'd lost them all. We had mostly rookies, and we played before crowds of 2,000. But ever so slowly, we rebuilt. We took players like Tony Armas and Doug Bair and Mitchell Page and Rick Langford and Doc Medich and molded them into a decent club. Two years after I left, Billy Martin took them to the playoffs.

I always used to tell Charlie whom to go after in trades. He'd ask, "How do you know?" and I'd say, "I managed these guys in the minors," or "I saw them play."

Still, I guess some of the things I did bothered him. When I didn't take Mitchell Page out in the sixth inning. . . . When I didn't take Earl Williams out. . . . When I didn't consider the squeeze. . . . When the guys weren't choking up. . . . And so on.

When I went to bed the night of June 9, 1977, our record was 26 and 27.

At 6 A.M., the phone rang.

"McKeon? It's Finley!"

"Hi, Charlie."

"Jack," he said, "I want to talk about baseball and about you. I've decided to make a change. I'm letting you go. Bobby Winkles is taking over. But, listen, I'd

like you to stay on as assistant general manager.
You'll be my right-hand man. Whaddya say?"

"Let me think about it Charlie," I said.

At 7:15 A.M., the phone rang.

"Decided yet?"

No, I hadn't. I told Charlie to give me a day. I drove
up to the wharf in San Francisco and saw the sights.
I wandered and wandered and finally decided, What
the hell, I'd take it.

The next day, Charlie already was grumbling
about Winkles. I sat in Charlie's box watching the
ball game, and Charlie was saying, "Why aren't these
guys stealing? What's the problem? What's going on
down there?"

I couldn't help it. I grinned a little and said,
"Those aren't my headaches anymore, Charlie. You
took them away from me."

I was supposedly Charlie's right-hand man, but I
wasn't, really. Hammer was.

Hammer was a young black kid Charlie had taken
a liking to. He was about 16 years old, and Charlie
made him vice-president. Hammer would sit up in
the box and answer the telephones while Charlie was
back in Chicago. Five minutes before every game,
Hammer would telephone Charlie back in Chicago
and give him the play by play. And Hammer was a
sharp kid because he knew exactly what Charlie
wanted to hear. For instance, maybe a rabbit would
be on first base and wouldn't try stealing second.
Hammer would say to Charlie, "Charlie! He didn't
go! He didn't go!"

And Charlie would get upset. He'd ask, "Why
didn't he run, Hammer?"

Other times, if one of our pitchers was having
trouble, Hammer would say, "Nobody's warming up

in the bullpen, Charlie! Nobody's warming up!"

And Charlie would yell, "Why isn't anyone warming up?"

The year I was Charlie's assistant, I'd see Hammer do this night after night. He'd give Charlie the play by play for the entire game: "The pitcher's looking in for the sign, Charlie. He's checking the runner, Charlie. He delivers! Oh, it's high and outside. Ball one! The count's 1 and 2, Charlie."

One night, Charlie wanted Hammer to run and get something out of his office, and he told Hammer to give me the phone. I grabbed the receiver and began talking to Charlie. He said, "What's going on in the ball game, Jack?"

I said, "Well, Charlie, the count is 1 and 1."

I'd pause for about 10 seconds, and I'd say, "Now it's 2 and 1, Charlie."

Charlie got angry.

"Hey Jack," he said, "what's going on?! You've got to learn how to broadcast, Jack! When Hammer gets back, I want you to sit down and listen to him and see how he describes the game! I want to hear things like, 'He's checking the runner and here's the pitch.' C'mon Jack. Hang around Hammer, and you'll get a little direction."

Every once in a while, Hammer would make a road trip, and he'd always be on the phone with Charlie. He knew exactly what Charlie wanted to hear. If the centerfielder didn't make a catch, he'd say, "Charlie, he should've had it! He should've had it!" I remember one game when we were winning, 9–0, and Joe Coleman, our pitcher, had a two-hitter. He walked a guy, and Hammer told Charlie, "He's losing it, Charlie! And nobody's up in the bullpen!"

Charlie would then have Hammer give me the

phone. And Charlie would say, "Jack! Go call Winkles and tell him to get Coleman outta there! You hear me!"

Anyway, after the season, I went to manage in Puerto Rico, which was nice for some comic relief. But one day, Charlie called me out of the blue (not at 6 A.M.), and asked me if I'd return to the field as Winkle's third-base coach. I thought that sounded good, but he wondered if I could get along with Winkles after he'd taken my job. I told him I'd be the best third-base coach Bobby Winkles ever had. And, listen, I knew what Charlie wanted on sacrifice flies.

"Back! Back! Back! Back! . . . Go! Go! Go! Go!"

The year was 1978, and I had a wonderful time coaching third. I'd wake up to alarm clocks, not phone calls. Not that I'd sleep past 6 A.M. They don't call me Geritol Jack for nothing.

Anyway, Charlie essentially left me alone but never let Winkles out of his sight. Winkles was going nuts, and one day during the season he quit. We all tried talking him out of it, but he wouldn't budge. But I knew why. I knew why.

That day, before the game, Red Schoendienst, Lee Stange, and I all looked at each other and then at the clock. Gametime was fast approaching, and Charlie hadn't named a new manager yet.

"Make out a lineup, Jack," somebody said.

"Hell no," I said. Red was the elder statesman, so I felt he should do it.

The phone rang suddenly, and the clubhouse guy said it was for Red. I figured it was Charlie on the phone, and I figured Red would end up replacing Winkles. I was glad. Red had managed a World Champion in St. Louis in 1967, and I thought he'd be a hell of a choice.

Red left and quickly returned, saying Charlie wanted to talk to me on the phone upstairs. I walked up to the offices.

"McKeon? It's Finley!"

"Hi, Charlie," I said, thinking there was something strangely familiar about this.

"Jack, let me read something to you, and you tell me how it sounds: 'Bobby Winkles has resigned today, and I am reappointing Jack McKeon as manager.' . . . Well, do you want the job?"

I actually paused for three seconds. Normally, I would've accepted it in one second, but I remembered how good a time I was having coaching third. Still, I figured Charlie would fire me on the spot if I didn't take the job, so I did.

The game began 20 minutes later, and we ended up losing, 2–1. Charlie never called me once during the game.

Afterward, my wife Carol couldn't believe I took the job. "You're only gonna get fired again," she said.

She was right.

Well, the day after my first game, Charlie flew me into Chicago to brief me on some new ground rules. He and his son picked me up to take me to Charlie's office, but Charlie stopped at a barbershop along the way. He wanted to have his hairpieces shampooed.

So he's got one hairpiece on his head and one in his hand, and I'm sitting there sort of dumbfounded. Charlie quickly introduced me to his barber.

"Sid, I want you to meet my new manager, Jack McKeon," Charlie said. "C'mon, Sid. Doll him up. Make him look like a big-league manager. Give him a big-league haircut. C'mon Jack, hop in that chair!"

I was gonna get a free $35 haircut, so I didn't

argue. I was sitting there getting my trim when
Charlie sent his son out to grab some cold cuts. The
kid came back with cheese and bologna and ham
and rye bread and mustard and mayonnaise, and
Charlie asked me what I wanted.

I didn't really care, but Charlie ended up handing
me a big double-decker sandwich. And I ate it, sitting
in a barber's chair with strands of hair falling all
over the rye bread. It wasn't one of my better meals.

Charlie, to tell the truth, wasn't much different the
second time around. He drafted two pitchers out of
high school and sent them to me immediately. We
were in the middle of a pennant race, and he was
handing me some 17 year olds. He wanted them in
the rotation, too.

I'm not saying they were bad kids. One of them
was Mike Morgan, who was taken No. 1 in the draft
out of Las Vegas High School. Charlie signed him to
a $25,000 contract with a guarantee that he'd pitch
right away in the big leagues. So Morgan was gonna
start against Baltimore. Charlie invited the kid's par-
ents, the kid's girlfriend, the kid's buddies, and the
kid's nextdoor neighbor. They all sat with Charlie,
and they cheered Morgan's every move.

The kid didn't do badly. The Orioles scored off
him in the second inning and put a couple runners
on in the fourth. I got the bullpen up.

Immediately, the dugout phone rang.

"McKeon? It's Finley!"

"Hi, Charlie."

"Jack, the boy's father says he's pitched nine innings, ten innings at a time in high school. He says
he can go longer than four innings. So, listen Jack,
tell the relievers to sit on down."

"You're the boss, Charlie," I said.

So we stayed with Morgan, and he fought his way out of the jam. We scored a run, but the Orioles took a 3-1 lead into the seventh. Morgan was struggling again. I got the bullpen up.

Immediately, the phone rang.

"McKeon? It's Finley!"

"Hi, Charlie."

"Listen, Jack. His father says he can definitely go nine innings. He says it's no problem. I know you'd normally make a change, Jack, but let him go nine."

"You're the boss, Charlie."

So everyone went home happy but me. The kid went nine, and we lost, 3-1.

Morgan's next start was in Baltimore, and Charlie made a special trip to see the game—minus the kid's father. Unfortunately, Morgan gave up four first-inning runs and then slipped while trying to field a ball in front of the mound, injuring his ankle.

Our trainer said the ankle was starting to swell, so I got Morgan out of there. Charlie—who was sitting in the front row nearby—wanted Morgan to stay in. He leaned over the railing and shouted, "Tell McKeon I want to see him!"

I walked over to his seat while my reliever warmed up.

"What the hell's going on?" Charlie asked.

"Kid's got a bad ankle," I said.

"So you took him out?" Charlie asked. "Hell, I flew here to see him pitch! You don't take him out without talking to me, you hear!"

I said, "From now on, I'll do that Charlie."

So a week later, Charlie sent me his No. 2 draft pick, Tim Conroy. Conroy, who was also 17, came out of a tiny school in Pennsylvania. Charlie insisted I give him the ball.

Conroy joined us in Kansas City, and we started him. Charlie hadn't flown in to see the game, and it's a good thing. We got five runs in the first, but the Royals pecked away and tied it up. I got the kid out of there in the fourth, and we ended up winning.

At that point, we finally sent both Morgan and Conroy to the minors, but the damage had been done. Our rotation had been thrown out of whack, and the team struggled thereafter. Morgan, of course, now pitches for the Seattle Mariners, and Conroy throws for St. Louis. Like I said, they weren't bad kids or bad pitchers. They were just too young.

The season mercifully ended, and I really thought the foundation was there for the future. They had kids like Rickey Henderson and Dwayne Murphy coming up through the minors, and we'd acquired Tony Armas and others. I figured we were only a couple years away, and I was right. Billy Martin took them to the playoffs in 1981.

As for me, I doubted Charlie would bring me back. My contract had expired after the 1978 season, and I still hadn't heard from him by December. At the winter meetings, Montreal's John McHale asked if I wanted to manage his Triple-A club in Denver, and it sounded pretty attractive. But I owed Charlie a courtesy call.

I told him he'd been good to me, and I offered to stay on with him, as a coach or whatever. Charlie sounded a little down. He said he was trying to sell the team, and he told me it might be best if I took the Denver job. He promised he'd call McHale and give me a hearty recommendation.

Before I hung up, I told Charlie that I was now one of three guys he'd hired and fired twice. The others were Alvin Dark and Hank Bauer, and I kind of wanted to be the record holder. So I asked Charlie if he'd hire me a third time that day and then fire me the following day. That way, I'd go down in Charlie Finley history as the only guy to be fired three times.

Alas, Charlie said it was a good idea and that he might have gone for it in other years. But he was trying to sell the club and figured it might be bad PR. So Charlie Finley and I hung up on each other one last time.

When I'd been fired in Kansas City, everyone in my family cried. And when Charlie fired me the first time, everyone cried.

But this time, Carol and the kids said, "Bye, daddy," and left for the beach.

I tell you, if I ever trade Tim Flannery, our second baseman, not only will I be run out of town, I'll be run out of my house. My wife loves the guy. Well, I tell you what. I'd trade Timmy, if the right deal came along.

11
Ray, Joan, Ballard, and Me

RAY AND JOAN Kroc—and don't forget Ballard Smith—brought me into their family in September of 1979. It was nice of them. I haven't been the same since.

What they did was get me off the field. I had spent that one season managing in Denver, but John McHale called me one day to say the San Diego Padres wanted permission to speak with me. My initial thought was, 'Who cares? I don't want to manage another lousy team.' But McHale told me to listen. He said it sounded like an offer I couldn't refuse.

I arrived in San Diego and met immediately with Bob Fontaine, who was the Padre general manager at the time. Bob asked me if I wanted to be his assistant. I'd work out of my home in North Carolina, I'd scout, and I'd help make trades.

Took me about 15 minutes to say yes.

See, I was burned out from managing. Charlie

Finley and Cedric Tallis and all the others had done it to me, not to mention a few players like Bill Faul and a few umpires like Joe Ring.

Besides, I sort of had this thing about making trades.

Fontaine immediately brought me into the picture. He said he was working on a deal with Cincinnati, and the Reds wanted one of his infielders, Kurt Bevacqua.

Kurt Bevacqua! Hell, I'd had Kurt in Kansas City back in 1974, and we ended up trading him to Pittsburgh that year. The Royals re-signed him in 1975, but then I got fired and he got released.

So now I show up in San Diego, and who's the first player I hear about? Bevacqua.

I did what came natural: I traded him to Pittsburgh.

My first Padre deal.

A year later, Bevacqua was out of a job again and called me up. We ended up re-signing him, and he played well in the 1984 playoffs and World Series. I had the guy four times in my career, which makes me kind of sick to think about.

One day in Kansas City I looked up in the first inning and saw Bevacqua—in uniform—selling posters in the stands. Unfortunately, it was a poster of himself, and nobody was buying.

I began scouting a number of American League teams for the Padres and then I went down to inspect the Padre farm system. For the first time, I was seeing guys like Eric Show and Mark Thurmond. After I'd seen Show pitch one day in El Paso, I gave Fontaine a call. He was in Los Angeles that day for the 1980 All-Star game, and his wife answered his hotel phone. She sounded a little curt, a little distant. I wasn't sure what was up, until Bob got on the phone and told me he'd been fired.

I gave him my condolences and asked him what was gonna become of me. It was July, and I'd only been on the job since September. I really didn't want to go. I liked what I was doing.

Bob told me to sit still and keep doing what I'd been doing. I flew back to North Carolina and was gonna watch the All-Star game on the tube when the phone rang. It was Ballard Smith. Ballard, the team president, wanted to chat.

We chatted. He wanted me out in San Diego as soon as possible. I took a late night flight and arrived the following morning. My luggage was lost, but not my bearings. I went down to the Padre clubhouse, took a shower, shaved, and went up to see Ballard.

He needed a favor. He needed me to stay on in an interim basis until they hired a new GM. In the meantime, I'd be in charge. He told me to make any trade I wanted, and I didn't even have to consult him. I could release anyone, sign anyone, do whatever I felt was best. It was my baby.

He asked me if I was at all interested in the full-time GM job. "Hell, yes," I said. But he told me I wouldn't get it. Ray, the owner, wanted a big name.

Gene Mauch and Charlie Fox were brought in and interviewed for the job. In the meantime, I was doing my best. We had guys like Rollie Fingers, Dave Winfield, Gene Tenace, Randy Jones, Bob Shirley, Ozzie Smith, Jerry Mumphrey, Gene Richards, Aurelio Rodriguez, John D'Aquisto, and Willie Montanez. A few of them were winners—Winfield and Smith—but some were older and needed to be dealt away. I peddled Montanez and D'Aquisto and got prospects in return. It was spring training, and I was giving my veterans to pennant contenders and getting quality in return.

I talked to the Yankees about Mumphrey. I was in Phoenix, and I was pleading for Ruppert Jones and a few other prospects. They didn't want to give me Jones; they wanted to give me Bobby Brown, who I later got anyhow. I persisted. I wanted Jones.

So, in the end, I traded Mumphrey and John Pacella to the Yankees for Jones, Joe Lefebvre, Tim Lollar, and Chris Welsh. Not bad.

As I look back, I remember they agreed to give us Jones and Lefebvre and Lollar, but I was holding out for another lefty pitcher—I can't remember who. But Charlie used to tell me, "McKeon! If you want to be a hog, you'll end up eating manure!" And that sometimes is the big holdup in trades. Guys want to be outright piggish. Me, I get deals done. So I settled for Welsh.

At home, my wife kept track of who had interviewed for the GM job. She told me Cedric Tallis— my old friend from Kansas City—had been considered, not to mention Lou Gorman. Carol kept pontificating about who they'd hire, but I said, "I'll get the job."

Hell, I didn't know. But I was gonna think positive.

About mid-September, Ballard called me to his office. Ray was in there with him. Ballard, who previously had said I had no chance for the job, put it in my lap. Ray said they'd interviewed a bunch of guys, but I was as qualified as all of them. And, hell, I'd already made some good deals.

"It's yours if you want it," Ray said.

I wanted it.

Listen, Ray Kroc was one of my all-time favorites.

Here's a guy who busted his rear end all his life to build the McDonald's empire. We were alike in a lot of ways. We both thought everyone in the world should take Geritol; we both smoked cigars.

Whenever I was in Ray's box alone, I wasn't allowed to light up. Other people in the box would say, "Nah. No smoking here." But as soon as Ray would walk in, I'd say, "Ray, you want a cigar?"

"Sure, Jack," he'd say.

And we'd both light up, and nobody would say a word. Hell of a guy.

People would send him real expensive cigars, cigars that cost $72 a box. He thought $72 cigars were too good for him to smoke, so he'd drop 'em off in my office. I'd smoke 'em.

Often, Ray would buzz my office and say, "C'mon down when you get a chance, Jack. We'll talk."

And I'd go down there at the end of a day, and he'd go over all my potential deals. Ray, he was a good man. He took care of his employees. That was his method of running a top organization. Whether it was McDonald's or the Padres, he'd slip his best employees big bonuses. Our morale in that office was great.

When Ray suffered a stroke and was bedridden for a while, I'd go visit him in the hospital, and he'd tell me all about his business, about how McDonald's was coming out with some new cookie. Up until his last season, 1983, he was extremely sharp. When it came to baseball, he was right on top of it. He'd sit in his box with me, and he'd say things like, "Look at our outfielder, Jack. He's playing way too deep." Or, "Jack, he should've caught that darn ball." Things an ordinary fan wouldn't have said. He'd scream, "Get rid of this guy! Send him to the minors!"

I'd tell him I couldn't, and he'd say "Why not?"

Ray didn't always know the rules, like the fact that you couldn't option certain players, but he really got fed up with some guys.

I remember Winfield misplaying a fly ball and Ray chanting, "Trade him! Trade him!" Or he'd yell, "Hustle, Winfield!" Or, "Jump, Winfield!"

One day in 1980, he pleaded with me to get rid of pitcher Randy Jones, the former Cy Young Award winner. But then he softened and said, "There's no way anyone will take him, right Jack?"

I said, "You never know, Ray." The Mets had had some interest in Jones, and I told Ray we might be able to peddle him.

"You're kidding, Jack!" Ray said. "You do that, and I'll give you your own McDonald's franchise. No way you can trade him. Who'd want him?"

Hell, I was 60 percent certain I could do it. I ended up getting rid of Jones but I never did get that McDonald's franchise.

The guy Ray really disliked was Lefebvre. Joe would strike out in key situations, and Ray would throw a fit. He'd call him a "stiff" and other stronger words. Then, one night, Lefebvre cracked a game-winning home run. Ballard couldn't resist. He turned toward Ray and said, "Who was the guy who hit the home run, Ray?"

"He's still a stiff," Ray said.

Ray Kroc, he was a good one. We really miss him.

In the meantime, we were slowly building a contender, even though we lost Winfield to free agency and ended up trading Ozzie Smith. A lot of people in San Diego can't understand losing those two, so let me explain.

Winfield's contract was up after the 1980 season,

and negotiations during that season turned out to be fruitless. By the end of the year, we knew we'd lose him. And I tell you, I did my best to make a deal, so we'd at least get something in return. At the 1980 World Series, the Yankees expressed interest in him. Back then, free agency wasn't such a guarantee. If a guy like Winfield filed, only 13 teams were allowed to claim him, and he'd have his choice among those 13.

Well, George Steinbrenner wanted Winfield pretty damn badly and wasn't sure he wanted to take any chances. What if the Yankees were the 14th team to claim him? They'd be out of luck. Steinbrenner was worried.

So at the 1980 Series, I talked to them about a trade. They would have the rights to Winfield, and in return I'd get either Joe Lefebvre (who was still with the Yankees then) or Steve Balboni (who hadn't been traded to the Royals yet) or an infielder named Pat Tabler. It all hinged on when Winfield filed. See, he was eligible to file as soon as the Series ended. But we couldn't do interleague trading until five days after the Series. Therefore, if Winfield waited five days to file, we would make the deal.

He didn't wait. He filed the night the World Series ended.

Hell, the Yankees got him anyway.

At least we tried.

As for the Ozzie Smith trade in 1981, it wasn't easy. Ozzie, as you know, was an inspiration to the community, the most popular guy around. Problem was, his contract was gonna be up in 1982, and we weren't confident we could sign him.

At the 1981 winter meeting, Ballard, our manager Dick Williams, and I talked about what we should do. St. Louis had approached us, and the Cardinals really liked Ozzie. And we really liked their shortstop, Garry Templeton.

Tempy had been the first switch hitter to collect 100 hits from each side of the plate in the same season. He and Whitey Herzog had had a falling out, but I like to give guys second chances. Usually, they turn out to be better.

So we made the deal. It came down to us getting Templeton, Sixto Lezcano, and Luis DeLeon for Ozzie and Steve Mura. We thought it was a hell of a deal: first of all, Tempy had been ten times the hitter Ozzie was. We needed someone who could hit, and we got that in Tempy and Lezcano. We needed a relief pitcher and we got DeLeon.

If we were trying to win popularity contests, we wouldn't have done it. But we tried to convey to the fans that this was all done to build a pennant winner. People could say we goofed. I don't. The Cardinals won the pennant with Smith; we won the pennant with Templeton. Hell, when I trade a guy, I hope he does well. A good trade helps both teams. Some of these GMs are so scared players will come back and haunt them. They're afraid to trade guys within their division.

I'm not. This last season, we traded pitcher Dave Dravecky to the Giants, who are in our division. Sure, I hated to do it. I wouldn't mind having Dave Dravecky for a son. I wouldn't mind having 25 Dave Draveckys on my team. But we had a chance to acquire Chris Brown, who we really liked, and a couple of young pitchers in Mark Grant and Mark Davis. I was sad to see Dravecky go, but I wasn't sad when he started pitching shutouts for the Giants and winning playoff games. You gotta have the guts to make trades, even if it means upsetting the community.

I tell you, if I ever trade Tim Flannery, our second baseman, not only will I be run out of town, I'll be run out of my house. My wife loves the guy. I remember Ballard Smith telling me his kids loved the guy, too. Well, I tell you what. I'd trade Timmy, if the right deal came along.

Listen, I always say you trade quality for quality. If you want a good player, you gotta give up a good player. The days are gone when you just rip somebody off. We're not here to embarrass other teams. We're here to help our own club.

In 1981, we helped ourselves by acquiring catcher Terry Kennedy from St. Louis. We had to get stronger up the middle, and I didn't have a competent catcher or second baseman. The catchers I wanted were either Kennedy or Pittsburgh's Tony Peña or Oakland's Mike Heath. I really tried getting Peña, but the Cardinal deal made more sense. St. Louis already had Ted Simmons behind the plate, and I was calling Whitey Herzog all the time, saying, "Give me Kennedy. What's your problem?"

I spent more time talking to Whitey than my wife. Carol's prettier, though.

Anyway, we finally made the deal at the winter meetings. The keys were sending Rollie Fingers, Gene Tenace, and Bob Shirley to St. Louis for Kennedy. People say we gave up entirely too much, but, hell, I needed a catcher, an All-Star catcher.

Charlie Finley always used to tell the story about the hammer and the nails. Let's say you go into a hardware store needing a hammer. The hammer usually costs $9.95, but on this particular day, it costs $19.95. You're mad. But then you look and see that nails are going for twenty cents a pound instead of $1 a pound. You say, "Wow." But you're there for the hammers, not for the nails. You need a hammer to complete your house, and you figure you have to pay more. You don't need any nails.

Well, that's how I felt about Kennedy. I figured I'd be better off paying more for a premium catcher. I was hoping he'd be an All-Star, and he was.

So, little by little, the team took shape. By 1984, we were on our way to the pennant. What a year. We had Kennedy behind the plate, and we'd signed Steve Garvey to play first base. We had Tempy at short, and we decided to move Alan Wiggins from the outfield to second base. We had drafted a kid named Kevin McReynolds and put him in center field. We had a second-year rightfielder named Tony Gwynn, one of the greatest kids I'd ever seen. We signed reliever Goose Gossage as a free agent, and we had pitchers like Eric Show, Mark Thurmond, Ed Whitson, and Tim Lollar.

Now I needed a leftfielder and a lefty in the bullpen. It was crazy how I got 'em.

At the 1983 winter meetings, I was shooting the breeze with Cub GM Dallas Green. That's usually how trades are made, by the way. You listen on the radio, you hear rumors, you hear whispers. So, I'm in Nashville for the winter meetings, and the Expos are interested in one of my pitchers, Gary Lucas. Hell, they wanted to give me pitcher Scott Sanderson, but that's not who I wanted. It looked like we weren't gonna do anything. But then I ran into Dallas Green.

I said, "How's it going, Dallas?"

He said, "Not so good." He needed a pitcher badly and wasn't having much luck. I milked him for information.

"So you got anybody in mind, Dallas?"

"Yeah," he said. "Sanderson."

My eyes got big.

"I can get Sanderson," I told him. "Hell, Dallas, I just turned him down. I can get him for Lucas."

He said, "How 'bout you get Sanderson and give him to me. What do you want for him?"

Well, it took me about five seconds to say, "Craig Lefferts and Carmelo Martinez."

Martinez was a top first baseman prospect who could maybe play the outfield. And Lefferts was a decent lefty. Exactly what we needed.

Of course, you're probably wondering why the Cubs didn't trade directly with Montreal. The best I can say is that Montreal had a different scouting report. They didn't see anybody on the Cubs they liked. Maybe the time they saw Lefferts, he got bombed. Or maybe the time they saw Martinez, he struck out. But I liked those two guys.

So I went back to Montreal and my old buddy John McHale, and said we might be able to make the Lucas-Sanderson deal. And I gambled a little. I said I'd only do it if he threw in Al Newman, an infielder. He agreed.

Then I came back to Dallas Green and said I needed one more player if I was gonna give him Sanderson. I wanted third baseman Fritz Connally, not to mention Martinez and Lefferts. He agreed.

So not only had I found my leftfielder and lefty reliever, I'd conned my way into getting two more guys.

Now, all I needed to complete our puzzle was a solid third baseman, a third baseman who could hit for power and play a little defense. Graig Nettles was available in New York.

Steinbrenner apparently felt I'd taken advantage of his people in the Mumphrey deal. So he refused to negotiate the Nettles deal directly with me. He said he would only talk to Ballard, and I really didn't give a hoot. Because when Ballard was speaking on the phone with George, I was sitting in a chair right next to Ballard. I told him exactly what to say and what to do and who to ask for.

We got Nettles for pitcher Dennis Rasmussen just days before the 1984 season, and I really thought the Nettles deal put us over the hump. Before we had him, there was no doubt in my mind we had a good chance to win the pennant. But when we got him, it psychologically lifted the ballclub. The players were thinking, "Hey, management's behind us. They're interested in winning." It was the icing on the cake. In my opinion, the day we acquired Nettles was the day we won the pennant.

And the 1984 season did turn out to be magical. Ray Kroc had died over the winter, and we dedicated the season to him. I wasn't allowed to smoke in his box anymore, but I lit up a victory cigar in early October. We won our division and then came back from a 2-games-to-none deficit to beat the Cubs in the playoffs.

I got a telegram from Steinbrenner. It said, "The lion's share of credit has to go to you. You were patient. You made some great moves. You took me to the cleaners. And I am happy for you. You should be very proud of the job you did. Sincerely, George Steinbrenner."

What else do I remember about 1984? We had the big beanball war in Atlanta that year and I thought it was completely uncalled for. I certainly didn't condone how Dick Williams had ordered our pitchers to hit Braves pitcher Pascual Perez when he came to bat. I sat in the stands that day worrying. Here we were, going for our first division championship, and Dick was instigating a beanball incident. We had everything to lose. I thought it showed a lack of common sense. Ridiculous. It really disturbed me. We got fined about $25,000 by Chub Feeney—who was the National League president at the time, although now he's the Padres' president—but we couldn't contest those fines. Feeney was right. Our players had orders from Dick to throw at Perez. And Perez, I'll tell you, was a pretty good dodger. Our pitchers couldn't hit him.

It was a strange year. We had to start the playoffs with reserve umpires, because of an umpire strike. It was kind of scary, but they finally got the strike settled.

Our experience in the World Series was also scary. We were in Detroit, and the place was a madhouse. The Tiger fans had gone berserk. We lost the series in five games, and we were all sitting trapped in a bus after Game Five. The streets were completely blocked. Cars were being set on fire, and rocks were being thrown at our bus. It was ugly.

Obviously, 1984 was special. It was the first Padre team to go to the World Series, and we were a part of that. They can't take it away. After all the years the good people of San Diego suffered, we finally won. People there deserved that World Series. It's a great place to play. The fans, I think, were very patient with us.

But I still wasn't completely content with that team. Eric Show and Mark Thurmond had gotten bombed in the playoffs and World Series, and we

needed a stopper in our starting rotation. So that
December at the winter meetings in Houston, I was
on the lookout for a pitcher. We had a pretty valuable
commodity in Ozzie Guillen, a minor-league shortstop who had a lot of Ozzie Smith's tendencies. We
were talking to the White Sox about Richard Dot-
son, and they were being stubborn. They offered me
Floyd Bannister, but I didn't want him. The deal
wasn't working.

I was hanging out in the hotel lobby, because that's
what I always do at winter meetings: mind my own
business on some comfortable couch and wait for
something interesting to happen. Roland Hemond—
the White Sox GM—came by and asked, "Got any
interest in LaMarr Hoyt?"

I was thinking "Hell, yes" but I couldn't let them
know that. So I said, "Uh, Roland, let me think
about it."

I had had no idea they'd be willing to trade Hoyt,
which is why I never asked for the guy. We eventually
met privately with Rollie and his people, and they
wanted Guillen and Tim Lollar and Luis Salazar. I
told them that was too much to give up for Hoyt. I
wanted someone else, and it looked like the deal was
gonna die. But then Ballard ran into Eddie Einsdorf,
the White Sox owner, and Eddie said, "Hey Ballard.
How come we can't get this done?"

So we met again, and they gave me some kids—
Kevin Kristan and Todd Simmons. (Simmons, by the
way, is still on our major-league roster.) In all, it
turned out to be a seven-player deal: Guillen, Lollar,
Salazar, and pitcher Bill Long for Hoyt, Christian,
and Simmons.

OK, OK. Guillen went on to become Rookie of the
Year, and LaMarr ended up in jail on drug charges.
So you say we screwed up, right? Wrong. LaMarr

gave us a good year in 1985 and was even the MVP in the All-Star game. He eventually hurt his shoulder and fell apart emotionally, but he was the guy we wanted. I have no regrets. At the time, it was a hell of a deal. If you really want to analyze it, losing him to drugs killed us. Losing Alan Wiggins to drugs killed us. And what I mean is we weren't able to trade either player. Our club policy at the time was to trade or release players who had been involved with drugs more than once. Consequently, we didn't get much in return because other teams knew we had little bargaining power. Wiggins was a guy who stole 70 bases in 1984, but we ended up trading him to Baltimore for pitcher Roy Lee Jackson, who didn't do much for us.

As for Hoyt, we just flat-out released him, getting zero in return. Certainly, he could've been the throw-in in some deal that could've gotten us a better player. But that's history now. I guess I can't worry about it.

So it just made it harder to rebuild. We lost two guys who had value, two guys we could've traded for someone of equal value or at least close to equal value. Instead, we had to get lucky. We had to hope that a guy like pitcher Jimmy Jones—one of our former No. 1 picks—or a guy like second baseman Bip Roberts would come through. We had to pray.

As it turned out, we never did replace Wiggins in 1985. We were in first place by half a game at the All-Star break, but we didn't play worth a nickel in the second half. There was the threat of a player's strike, and Dick Williams told the team to play each game as if it were their last, just in case of the strike. Not that it was his fault, but the team immediately went down the tubes.

No one took charge that year, not Dick or anyone.

There were a couple times I wanted to go down to the clubhouse and get all over the team. They were coasting, complacent after winning in 1984. But I felt that it wasn't my job. I felt that was the manager's job, and I'm one of those GMs who leave the manager alone. Sure, I talk a lot to Larry Bowa, our current manager, but that's because he seeks my opinion. I don't force my opinions down his throat.

As for Dick Williams, we are supposedly feuding now, but I always felt we got along. Dick and I communicated well. If he wanted my thoughts, he'd come get them. He was a good manager.

The problem with Dick was that he stopped communicating. He was the perfect manager for two or three years, but then he started having problems with players. Guys like Kevin McReynolds and Terry Kennedy were fed up with his so-called tough-guy image. It just wasn't working.

I guess Dick saw the writing on the wall, because after the 1985 season he indicated he didn't want to manage the team anymore. He said he didn't want to deal with the players or the media anymore. He told Ballard and me he was quitting. He told a lot of people he was quitting.

But we didn't announce it right away, which created major problems. Ballard wasn't able to reach Joan Kroc—who had taken control of the team after Ray died—and until he did, Dick wasn't officially gone. Ballard told Dick to think about whether he really wanted to quit, and to get back to him.

In the meantime, I figured I'd better give Dick's third-base coach, Ozzie Virgil, a chance to find a job. Obviously, our new manager would want to bring in his own third-base coach, so I called Ozzie in Venezuela and told him that for reasons I couldn't explain, we weren't going to renew his contract. But if anything changed, I'd let him know. I was only trying to be fair to the guy.

In the meantime, Ozzie's wife leaked it to the press that Ozzie had been fired, and that Ballard and I had done it to force Dick out. Joan read this in the paper, didn't fully understand what had happened, and said she was siding with Dick. Well, to make a long story short, everything erupted because Ballard hadn't been able to reach Joan to tell him that Dick had quit. It's nobody's fault, but that's what happened.

So Joan called a meeting to see what was going on. Did Dick really want to manage? Did he want to quit? Joan brought all of us over to her home in December of 1985.

Well, Dick had clearly told us before that he was gonna quit, and I asked him about it at Joan's meeting. I said, "Dick, I didn't think I had to consult you about Ozzie if you'd already said you'd quit." And he agreed.

Yet he later said I tried forcing him out. I'm not sure what he means.

So right now, I guess we're feuding. He calls me "Traitor Jack," and says I forced him out because I wanted to manage the team. Is he crazy or what?

I was still burned out from managing. Ballard and I never sat down and discussed any new managers. And I certainly wasn't a candidate, despite what people said. I promise you, I will never manage the San Diego Padres.

Listen, Ballard had asked me to manage as far back as 1981, before Dick came along. I told Ballard to let me sleep on it for a night, and I came back the next morning and said no. He decided to let Frank Howard continue as manager.

I never campaigned to manage that club. But Dick swears I did, and the media has brought it up, too. When they read about all that stuff about Charlie Finley, they'll figure out why I stayed away.

As for Dick, I've never had anything against the guy. What transpired in San Diego was a business decision, not a personal attack. Dick has been fired many times, and so have I. Sometimes teams do things for their own best interest. That's what happened in San Diego.

To this day, you've never heard me rip Dick, and I won't in this book. So that's that.

In 1986, everything went wrong again, and it became clear that we were going to have to rebuild just as we'd done in 1980 and 1981 and 1982 and 1983. We had to make decisions. Should we sit back and say, "We'll get one more fling out of these older guys"? Or should we say, "Let's make adjustments now"?

I figured we'd make adjustments, especially while we still had a good nucleus in Tony Gwynn and Garry Templeton and Steve Garvey and Tim Flannery.

So, first of all, we traded Terry Kennedy to Baltimore. We had the young kid Benito Santiago waiting in the wings, and we felt it was time to go with youth. Terry had given us what I thought he had to give. He was an All-Star for us. He struggled on defense, but we knew he would. He served his purpose. And look at what Santiago did in his place. He set the record for the longest hitting streak by a rookie, at 34 games. He hit .300 and won many post-season honors.

We also didn't bring back Nettles for 1987, and we released some veterans, Jerry Royster and Dave La-Point. We also traded Kevin McReynolds, who had led the club with 26 homers and 96 RBIs in '86.

OK, OK. People see McReynolds doing well in New York and say, "How could you do that, Jack?" Let me explain. During that '86 season, we were swiftly going down the tubes, and the Mets had called about McReynolds. Mac was basically an untouchable at the time. We had drafted him out of the University of Arkansas and he batted nearly .400 one year in the minors. He'd had a poor year in '85, but I feel part of that was due to Williams's mishandling of him. Under Steve Boros in '86, he was killing the ball.

Still, he had his inconsistent moments, too. He wasn't an excitable kid, the rah-rah type. Just by his nature, it sometimes looked like he was dogging it. I wasn't all that worried about it, though, because I knew I could motivate the kid. I'd give him some Geritol or something.

But when the Mets called and sounded so anxious to get him, I started thinking a bit. Lenny Dykstra, one of their young centerfielders, was my kind of kid. This kid took Geritol. He'd play hurt and dive for balls and so on. Here, finally, was a leadoff guy to replace Wiggins.

I told Frank Cashen, the Mets' GM, that there may come a time when I would trade McReynolds. I told him, too, that he wouldn't come cheaply, but we'd talk about it. In the meantime, I wished his team luck (they were about to make the playoffs) and said to keep in touch. I began scouting their players.

The Mets went on to win the World Series, and Cashen was asking me about McReynolds even then. Here they were playing the Red Sox, and he was thinking about next year.

In the meantime, Dykstra was playing great ball. I

really thought I had a chance of getting him, but when he started hitting home runs and making super catches, the chances grew slim. By the end of the Series, he was an untouchable.

So I didn't think much about trading with the Mets anymore. Heading into the 1986 winter meetings, my priority was to secure a third baseman. Nettles was too old, and I needed someone to play there. I went after Cleveland's Brook Jacoby and Montreal's Tim Wallach and Minnesota's Gary Gaetti and San Francisco's Chris Brown and Oakland's Carney Lansford. Nothing worked. Hell, Cleveland needed pitching and I had some to give them. But they wouldn't budge. I wanted to trade a pitcher to get my third baseman, but I had no luck.

Plan B was to get my third baseman with McReynolds. But if I was gonna trade Mac, I'd need a lot more than a third baseman. I wanted pitching, I wanted a centerfielder, and some more. At the winter meetings, I didn't talk to the Mets for the first two days. I was still hoping Plan A would work.

The third day, though, one of the New York sportswriters came to me and said, "The Mets say you don't want to talk with them."

"Whaddya mean?" I said. "That ain't true. If I've got someone they want, I don't think it's my job to go to them. I'm not campaigning to trade McReynolds. They gotta come to me."

Two hours later, they came to me.

Well, I shot for the works. Of course, I needed a third baseman, and I asked for Kevin Mitchell. I also asked for two of their better young pitchers: Rick Aguilera and Randy Myers. They said no to the pitchers. I asked again. They said no. I kept asking.

I was asking for too much, I know. I'd given them

a list of seven players I wanted, but I figured if I could get three of the guys on the list, I'd be doing all right. I needed to get at least three. So I kept plugging.

Well, when they wouldn't budge on Myers and Aguilera, I shifted to some other names, such as outfielders Stan Jefferson and Shawn Abner. And I still wanted some pitching, too.

One night, we went up to negotiate and I forgot my cigar. I felt naked. When I negotiate, I need my cigar. I need to be able to blow smoke—literally and figuratively. Sometimes, I even give out cigars to the other teams when I talk trades. Once I was negotiating with Jerry Kapstein, the agent for Steve Garvey and Goose Gossage and a bunch of others, and I offered him a cigar.

"Phew!" Kapstein said. "This cigar is strong. It'll wipe me out."

That's why I do it. It's my knockout punch.

Anyway, there was no way I was gonna make a deal without my cigar.

The next day, I met with the Mets again and I had a cigar. They weren't about to do any 3-for-1 deals. They wanted one of my lefty relievers, Gene Walter. Hell, I wasn't gonna do a 3-for-2. So I wanted some of their minor-league pitching. I asked for two kids: Kevin Armstrong and Kevin Brown.

They said that was too much. I said, "What the hell do you want?"

They wanted some minor leaguer. "Who?" I said. "Adam Gi—"

"You got him!" I snapped. They were asking for Adam Ging, an infielder we had. And I agreed before they even finished saying his name.

So that was that. McReynolds turned out to have a

hell of a year in 1987, but we got what we wanted. Jefferson has potential, and Abner could be a super- star. We ended up trading Mitchell to San Francisco for a third baseman we liked better: Chris Brown. So essentially we gave up a 27-year-old McReynolds, a proven player, to acquire three very good young players. And Brown had already been an All-Star.

I liked that trade.

Unfortunately, some people take trades the wrong way. McReynolds, for instance, was bitter at our or- ganization. He had taken a Padre duffel bag home with him over the winter of 1986, and when we traded him, we sent him a letter asking for payment for the bag—something like 37 bucks. Hell, that's standard treatment. He could send the bag back or he could pay for it. That was policy.

Well, Kevin ended up writing me a nasty letter. I'm sorry he felt that way. I liked the guy, and still do. What can I say?

So we'd built a whole new team for ourselves enter- ing the 1987 season. We even got a new manager.

His name was Larry Bowa. Larry had been a hell of a player, one of these guys who showed up for early batting practice every day and never skipped infield practice. He had a temper, too.

Before the 1986 season, we'd had an opening for a Triple-A manager. Larry had been offered a guaran- teed player contract with the Mets, but he turned it down because he wanted a managing job. He called Tom Romenesko, our farm director, and asked to interview for our Triple-A job.

Tom chatted with Larry and liked him instantly. Larry was living in Clearwater, Florida, at the time, and I happened to be on my way down there for a general manager's meeting. We decided to meet for lunch.

We sat there for four hours, and I enjoyed every minute. In a lot of ways, he was like me. Someone had given him Geritol, too. He had fight, this desire to work his butt off. He impressed me by saying he'd appreciated all the help his former managers had given him. He realized that a manager's job was to work with kids and get inside their heads. I knew then that he was the man for our job.

At first, when he managed at Triple-A Las Vegas, he was a ticking bomb. He said terrible things to umpires, most notably a female ump named Pam Postema. He got suspended twice. He kicked dirt at a particular ump and dust got in the ump's eye. The ump had to miss a week of action.

By mid-season, though, he really knew his players. And then, his team began winning like crazy. They went on to win the Pacific Coast League championship. So when the Padres needed a manager for the 1987 season, Larry was my choice. Sure, he could've used another year at Triple-A, but we had a young team now, and maybe he was just the guy we needed. A hardass.

He started out like a maniac. He took each loss personally. But soon, he got a grip on the team, and then we started scoring a few runs, which always helps.

Larry and I had a good relationship. He'd call me up for advice, but I wouldn't force myself on him. I didn't second-guess him at all. That's not me. I first-guess. I sit up in the press box while the game is going on and decide what I'd do in that situation. I don't wait until something goes wrong to say, "Oh I would've done it different." That's not me. When I was managing the Atlanta Crackers, a writer for the Atlanta *Constitution* second-guessed one of my pitching changes, in print. The next night, I was about to change pitchers, but I called this writer in the press box first.

"Hey, why don't you tell me who to bring in now and not tomorrow morning? First-guess me, don't second-guess me."

He didn't know what to say.

Anyway, before the 1987 season, Joan decided to sell the Padres. I was a little concerned about it, but then she changed her mind. In the meantime, Ballard—who probably was the scapegoat for all of our problems—stepped down as team president. It was kind of sad.

Ballard meant well. When I first met him, I thought he was an up-and-coming executive who was just beginning to take an active role in the club. This was 1979. Every deal I made, I ran it by Ballard. He always told me to do what I thought was best, but I owed him the courtesy of telling him.

Chub Feeney took over for Ballard during the '87 season, and I like Chub. He wanted to take a more active role in trades, which was fine with me. He is more of a hands-on team president. Ballard didn't get involved as much. Hell, I didn't mind. I appreciated Chub's input.

Our big trade came late in the '87 season, when we sent Dravecky, Mitchell, and Lefferts to the Giants for Chris Brown, Mark Grant, Mark Davis, and Keith Comstock. We never thought they'd give us Brown, but when they said they would, we had to give them quality in return. That's how this business works.

Like I said, I'm not in this business to rip people off. I'm here to smoke cigars and make a trade or two.

Let's say the Dodgers are talking to the Mets, and the Dodgers like the Mets' Howard Johnson, but the Mets don't like any of the Dodgers. And let's say the Mets like one of my guys. I can easily get Johnson from the Mets and then turn around and trade him to the Dodgers for somebody I want. If it sounds complicated, maybe it is.

12
Trader Jack
(Let's Talk Philosophy)

LISTEN, I'LL MAKE a deal any old time. At the 1980 winter meetings, I made one while checking out of my hotel. I was standing in line behind some lady when Detroit's GM Bill Lajoie came by and said, "Who do you want for Dennis Kinney?"

"What ya got for me, Bill?" I said.

He mentioned some outfielder I liked, and I said, "Good, we got a deal."

Then I checked out.

I guess that's my philosophy in a nutshell. You listen to the whispers and you hang around other baseball people and you read the newspapers and hear what you can.

At the winter meetings, I usually grab some couch in the lobby and call it my office. Other GMs walk by, and I say, "Step into my office, fella." A lot of sportswriters have told me that Whitey Herzog and I are the most fun at the winter meetings. They know

179

that Whitey and I will act on our impulses. Other GMs, they talk a good game, but that's it. Just talk.

If I sit in a room with Whitey, I can make a deal, any deal. I guarantee you. At the 1985 World Series, we snuck around a corner somewhere and started going at it.

Whitey: "Whaddya want for Kennedy?"

Me: "Gimme Andy Van Slyke and Ricky Horton, and I gotta have a catcher, too. So give me Tom Nieto."

Whitey: "Got it. We'll do it after the World Series."

We would've gotten it done, too, but Whitey wasn't the Cardinals' general manager. After the World Series, I approached Dal Maxvill, who *was* the Cardinal GM, and said, "Do you want to do what Whitey and I talked about?"

Maxvill said, "I'm not doing that deal, Jack."

"Hell," I said, "Whitey's the one who started it."

Maxvill said, "I'm the GM, and Whitey doesn't make the trades. I can't give you Van Slyke or Horton."

Whitey and I would've gotten it done, I'm telling you.

At the winter meetings, a lot of baseball people come to my couch if their deals with other clubs aren't working out. That's because a lot of times, I can help them out. I like to make three-way trades.

Let's say the Dodgers are talking to the Mets, and the Dodgers like the Mets' Howard Johnson, but the Mets don't like any of the Dodgers. And let's say the Mets like one of my guys. I can easily get Johnson from the Mets and then turn around and trade him to the Dodgers for somebody I want.

If it sounds complicated, maybe it is.

Let me give a real life example. In 1983, I got this

call from the Milwaukee Brewers, who were interested in Joe Lefebvre. They asked if I'd trade him,
and I knew Ray Kroc wouldn't have minded. I said
sure.

The Brewers then asked if I had any interest in
Yankee shortstop Bucky Dent. I said, "Not really,"
but I was curious. I asked them if they could really
get Dent from the Yankees, and they assured me they
could.

Well, if that was the case, I wasn't about to say no. I
told them I might take Dent. Why? Hell, I didn't need
a shortstop, but I could get Dent and turn around
and trade him. That's why it usually does no good to
say no. You never know what you can do.

So I got on the phone immediately. I called a couple of clubs that needed shortstops. I was shopping
Dent around, and I didn't even have him yet. Hell,
the Brewers didn't have him yet.

I called the Mets. They needed a shortstop badly,
but the Yankees certainly weren't gonna trade Dent
across town. So I could help the Mets out. Milwaukee
would get Dent; I'd trade Lefebvre for Dent; I'd give
Dent to the Mets.

But then, what would I get out of this? Well, I sort
of liked this young relief pitcher the Mets had, a guy
named Jesse Orosco. And I liked another of their
pitchers, a guy named Mike Scott.

The Mets said they'd think about it. In the meantime, the Brewers were getting itchy. They called me
back and said, "Well, you gonna give us Lefebvre?
We gotta know now."

I asked for an hour. I called the Mets back, and
they were hemming and hawing. They weren't sure
what to do. I told them I couldn't mess around all
night and that I wasn't gonna hold onto Dent just for

them. In a way, I was forcing them to panic. But they didn't. Shucks, I tried. The deal was off.

But, what I'm saying is you never, ever, ever tell someone you're not interested. You always try to see who else is available, and maybe you can work out a bigger deal.

Another thing I've learned is to get off my duff and do a lot of scouting. Sure, I have scouts in my system who are very competent, but if I'm gonna have the final say on a deal, I want to know what I'm getting and what I'm not getting. If you rely solely on your scout, you can get burned.

In 1981, the Yankees offered me a Double-A outfielder named Willie McGee. I said, "Willie who?" I'd never seen the guy. He had played consecutive seasons at Double-A Nashville, and the reports on him weren't that good. So I listened to my scouts and said no, and the kid ended up going from Double-A to Rookie of the Year with St. Louis. I saw what he did in 1982, and I got fed up as hell. His speed alone should've made him a prospect.

In 1982, Seattle had interest in one of my catchers, Ron Tingley. I was gonna let them have him, and they offered me a third baseman–outfielder named Jim Presley. I talked to my minor-league directors and my Triple-A manager and my scouts, and it looked like Presley was a decent hitter, but wasn't a good infielder or outfielder. He was destined to be a DH, and we don't have those in the National League. We turned him down.

Jim Presley's now an All-Star third baseman.

Alright, I'm not saying my scouts were wrong, but when you put 100 percent faith in them, it's your hide, not theirs. Point is, you gotta get around and see as many kids as you can.

Nowadays, John McHale of the Expos calls me all
the time, just to ask me about certain kids. He says,
"If anyone knows, it's you, Jack." I appreciate that,
but it's only because I get off my duff. I've said that
all along.

Evaluating talent is a kooky thing. Some have a
knack, some don't. I remember when I was managing in the minors, John Quinn was the Phillies'
general manager and his son, Bob, was my GM. At
the time, the Phillies were giving Curt Flood to the
Cardinals, and they wanted someone from the Cardinals' Triple-A team in Tulsa. I'd managed against
that club, so Bob had his dad John call me.

"Who do you like off that Tulsa club, Jack?" he
asked.

Well, I liked a kid named Willie Montanez, but
John said, "Didn't he break his leg last season?"

Yes, I said, but he was a hell of a player before he
broke it. He'd killed us with home runs. So I told
him he might be able to get him cheaply. I also told
him I liked a lefty named Jerry Reuss and another
pitcher named Reggie Cleveland.

You've probably heard of them.

Later with the Padres, I was trying to make a deal
with Pittsburgh, and I was looking particularly for a
catcher. This was right before we got Kennedy from
the Cardinals.

Well, I had my eye on the Pirates' Junior Ortiz and
the Phillies' Ozzie Virgil, now with the Braves. I
went up to Reading, Pennsylvania, to see them play
against each other, and I noticed a young left-handed
pitcher for the Pirates. He had good control and
knew how to pitch. He was crafty. I looked up his
name.

Dave Dravecky.

You try not to forget names. You just never know what'll happen down the road.

So the next winter, the Pirates called and were interested in one of our Triple-A outfielders, Bobby Mitchell. In return, they gave me a list of three names I could choose from: an outfielder, an infielder, and some pitcher named Dravecky.

Our farm director asked me what I thought, and I said, "Ah, take the pitcher. He seems like he kind of knows how to pitch. If we're lucky, we'll get ourselves a good Triple-A pitcher."

Two years later, Dravecky was in the big leagues. You might have heard of him, too.

Another time, I went up to see our Class-A team in Reno, where they were playing the Lodi Dodgers. This one kid for the Dodgers was a terror on the bases. He bunted for a hit, stole second, stole third, and scored. Next time up, he singled, stole second, stole third, and scored.

Alan Wiggins.

So at the minor-league draft that winter, I was looking for a sleeper, someone a team might not protect. I skimmed the list of unprotected players, and the last name on it was Wiggins.

I said, "Wiggins? Wiggins? Where have I heard this name!"

Didn't take me long to remember.

Two of my scouts said he wasn't a prospect, but I thought differently. Of course, the rule was that if we drafted him, we had to keep him on our big-league roster. He wasn't ready for the big leagues, but it was either that or ship him back to the Dodgers. Fortunately, we worked out a deal with the Dodgers and sent him to Triple A.

A year later, he was my leadoff hitter.

You win some, you lose some. But, as I've said, you've gotta find some guts inside your gut. I learned a lot—believe it or not—from my father. I learned about street smarts and a little about conning people. Hell, when I was a kid, I once traded a Foosball game for a pony cart. My father did a lot of trading like that. He'd trade tires for slot machines and rifles for gasoline.

He traded cars from his garage, too. I remember him trading this one lemon for a hell of a good car. I don't know how he did it. In those days, I guess you could rip people off.

In baseball, it ain't so easy.

Kelly, age six, was my batboy, and my second pitcher walked a bunch of guys and threw a couple of wild pitches. Kelly screamed out, "Skip, you better get him outta there. He's walking the ballpark."

13
The Wife and Kids
(I Couldn't Have
Managed Without You)

LET'S HEAR IT for baseball wives. They're the ones who hold your hand when you lose. They're the ones who scream at the umpires after you've been kicked out. They're the ones who babysit the kids while you're babysitting the ballplayers.

My wife, Carol, has been an inspiration.

Let's hear it for the baseball moms, too. And for the baseball girlfriends. It ain't easy being them. In the minors one year, a mother called me to say that one of my players was keeping her daughter out past midnight. And that was way too late. I told her that my player had a 1 A.M. curfew, and that maybe it was her girl who was keeping my player out.

"Well, I can't do a thing with her," the mother said. "She's too stubborn. I was hoping you could control your player!"

Another time, in Wilson, North Carolina, I got a frantic call at 2 A.M. from one of my players. He said that one of our pitchers had gotten a "Dear John" letter from his girlfriend and was gonna commit suicide.

"Skip," he said, "can you help?"

I roamed through the dark streets for hours and then later found him in bed sleeping off a hangover.

Another time, some girl barged into my office asking me to help her get back together with one of my ballplayers. Apparently they'd had a nasty fight.

"Honey, I'm not Don Cupid," I said. "It's between you and him."

She snapped, "Listen, if you don't help, I'll slash my wrists."

That's all I needed. I went and found my player, and he said not to worry—she threatened to slash her wrists twice a week.

"Sometimes she puts nicks in herself, Skip," he said. "But she's still here, isn't she?"

Another girl called me up with the question, "Has my boyfriend bought me the diamond ring he promised?"

I said, "How am I supposed to know?"

She said, "Well, I thought he had to check with you first."

Some baseball wives don't put up with a lot of garbage. I remember having this young kid with great tools. Great arm, great bat, great jokes in the dugout. All of a sudden, he stopped hitting, stopped playing defense, and stopped telling jokes. He didn't give a hoot if we won either. He was listless.

I finally said, "What's your problem, kid?"

It was his wife. She wanted him to quit baseball. And to make sure he did, she wouldn't cook for him and wouldn't sleep with him. And he finally quit.

Another time, I had this pitcher who liked to keep

his hair long. I personally don't care if you have it down to your shoulders, as long as you are doing your job. And this kid had a hell of a fastball, so I never said a word.

But it started getting ridiculous. During his wind-up, the hair would get in his eyes, and he'd throw balls in the dirt. I told him, "It's either the barber or a fine."

He took the fine. His wife wanted his hair long.

And I kind of understood. These women put up with so much. So many road trips, and so many late hours. And what if you have kids? I spend more time now with my grandkids than I ever did with my own children. Usually, you'd spend time with them in the off-season, but I was always down managing in Puerto Rico.

So I'd try to bring them to the park with me in the summer. Kelly, my oldest boy, was my ballboy most of the time. He got a kick out of it.

He also picked up all the right jargon. We had this pitcher named Billy Champion, whose record was pretty good. One day Kelly walked up to Billy and said, "What's your record?"

"15 and 3," Billy said.

Kelly said, "You? You're kiddin' me."

Kelly was six at the time.

Once I was managing an exhibition game in High Point, North Carolina, and I wanted to take a look at three of my pitchers. So I had each guy throw three innings.

Kelly, still age six, was my batboy, and my second pitcher walked a bunch of guys and threw a couple of wild pitches.

Kelly screamed out, "Skip, you better get him outta there. He's walking the ballpark."

Another day at High Point, I held a team meeting to lecture the guys about missing cutoff men. And I had singled out one of my players, a guy nicknamed Greenie.

We went out and played, and one of my outfielders, Jimmy Clark, missed his cutoff man. When the inning ended, I didn't say a word to him, but Kelly—age six—snapped, "You're just like Greenie, Jimmy."

Then again, I think Kelly put a lot of unnecessary pressure on himself because of me. He was playing an American Legion game once and had doubled to right field. I hadn't seen the hit, but I drove up in my car a few minutes later when he was still standing on second. I walked in and sat down, and he saw me. He froze. He became paralyzed. He wanted so badly to impress me that he just stood there.

He got picked off second. So I left.

So I'm here to say that I appreciate everything my wife and kids have done. I couldn't have managed without them.

Now that I'm in a front office and not a dugout, I see my girls Kristi and Kori and my boys Kelly and Kasey all the time. Of course, who's to say I won't manage again? I mean, I really enjoy being a general manager and all, but once you've managed in the big leagues, you always kind of want to go back. The thing I like about the GM job is that you control your own destiny. You're not at the mercy of 25 players and a general manager, too.

On the other hand, if the right situation comes up, everyone likes the challenge of managing. Not that I'm burned out of this GM job yet, but everybody gets burned out sometime. I'd like to stay in San Diego if they want me to and if they continue to let me have the proper input on trades. But if I don't have the input or can't do the things I've been accustomed to doing, I'd have to do some serious thinking.

In the last few years, three or four teams have approached me about managing, but I didn't want to leave this Padre job undone. I'm no quitter.

You know, I've watched my kids and I've noticed how my attitudes rub off on them. Kelly, for instance, is always reading the papers, always paying attention to what the Padres do. And I remember him bitching at me because we didn't sign Tim Raines as a free agent last winter.

He said, "You guys are gonna stink without Raines! What's your problem! Get him! Get going! Get off your duff!"

I was glad to see that Kelly finally had taken some Geritol.

Everybody should.

For your free catalog of Trader Jack memorabilia contact:

Imprinted Products Corporation
4669 Murphy Canyon Road
San Diego, CA 92123

Include your name, address, and phone number. Allow 2-3 weeks for delivery. For faster service call: (619) 541-1100.
Trader Jack memorabilia available: T-shirts, corduroy hats, lapel pins, brass key chains, ceramic mugs, and more!!